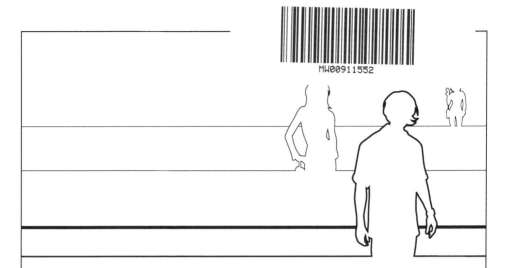

CONNECTED CULTURE

THE ART OF COMMUNICATING WITH THE DIGITAL GENERATION

WWW.CONNECTEDCULTUREBOOK.COM

JERRY ALLOCCA

Connected Culture:
The Art of Communicating
With the Digital Generation

Book Design by Atomic Wash
www.atomicwash.com

Library of Congress Control Number: 2011900267

ISBN 978-0-9831363-7-8

Printed in the United States of America

THIS BOOK IS DEDICATED TO **YOU:**

Who have supported and believed in me, who have enhanced my life and from whom I continue to learn. You, who were so generous in sharing the wisdom that has been critical to the success of the concepts in this book.

Thank you.

TABLE OF CONTENTS

INTRODUCTION

As I speak these words into my iPad's dictation app and watch it convert my voice into text for this book, I know the world has changed in a big way.

Just a few decades ago, traditional advertising worked like crazy. Companies like P&G built an empire by buying traditional advertising, like TV and radio spots, to build their brands. When there was less clutter on supermarket shelves and fewer products for customers to choose from, traditional advertising was the way to go. It was a money machine. All you had to do was feed it money (by buying more ads) and those ads generated more profit than it cost to advertise.

Boy, has marketing changed since then.

Today, the landscape is enormous; there is an explosion of products, services and choices. There is too much clutter. Traditional ads often get lost in the shuffle. And if they don't get lost, they're perceived as an interruption.

"THE CUSTOMER IS NOW MORE 'IN CONTROL' THAN EVER."

AND NOW A WORD FROM OUR SPONSOR...

The old way of interrupting the customer while reading the newspaper or watching television doesn't work as well as it used to. The Connected Culture has become very good at tuning out all the noise. They have to.

Being bombarded daily by advertising noise has made the Connected Culture very good at wearing combat helmets that keep out the danger of constant noise. They only let in what's relevant to them.

Today, you need to literally "connect" with your audience: you need relevance and you need their permission. You need trust. Marketing is evolving from a mass broadcast of one to many...into a one-on-one conversation focused on a topic that is of interest specifically to your customer.

THINK OUTSIDE THE BOX

Or better yet, think INSIDE the box. That "box" that is a part of the Connected Culture's everyday life: the computer (whether it's the computer that sits on your desk at work, at home or the one you carry in your pocket to make phone calls).

Thinking inside the box is one of the best ways to reach people today... if you do it right.

Today's best marketing techniques, most relevant messages and most welcome conversations take place online.

When someone joins a discussion group or interest group, you know at least one topic they're interested in. You know what they want to talk about. When someone types something into a search engine, they know what they want. They're telling you what they want. To get their attention you only need to give them what they're already asking for.

Being part of the Connected Culture lets you be more customer-centric than ever before. I challenge you to find any organization that says they're NOT customer-centric. But saying it and proving it on a daily basis are two completely different things.

Today, you have the ability to take your customer-centricity to incredible new levels. You can give the Connected Culture exactly what they want...become "the perfect fit"...because using the tools of the Culture, you will know exactly what they're looking for.

Reach people on their time, in the way they prefer. You don't have to wait for someone to read the paper, or tune in to the radio, or watch TV. It's not an interruption. It is what they want, and when they want it.

The old way of broadcasting messages was a one way street. Interactive media is a two-way street. Thanks to this new ability to interact, conversations are always possible between you and your prospective and existing customers. Now you can listen and respond to your customers anytime, anywhere.

"YOUR CUSTOMERS ARE TALKING ONLINE. ARE YOU LISTENING?"

— JERRY ALLOCCA

CONNECTED CULTURE

If you are active on a social network, then you are among the rapidly growing Connected Culture. Being part of this culture means you are connected with a group of people who use digital media as a way to communicate with one another.

If your organization is not yet actively involved in digital marketing, and you want it to be, this book aims to bridge the gap for you; to guide you in communicating with today's digital generation.

The Connected Culture doesn't open up an encyclopedia to do research for a paper; they don't generally open the newspaper to look for a job or conduct research for a work project. They "Google" the information they're interested in. Text messages and instant messages have quickly overtaken the number of phone calls the Connected Culture makes in a day. They connect daily through social media sites like Facebook, Twitter and LinkedIn. The digital generation uses media and devices that allow them to connect and socialize with one another at a moments' notice.

THE CONNECTED CULTURE IS ANYONE WHO USES DIGITAL COMMUNICATIONS ON A DAILY BASIS, AS PART OF THE WAY THEY RECEIVE INFORMATION AND CONNECT WITH PEOPLE.

THIS COULD BE YOUR 70 YEAR OLD UNCLE, OR HIS 20 YEAR OLD GRANDCHILD.

The digital generation grew up with digital communications. But no matter what age your targets are, they are frequent users of technology.

You can successfully market to your targets using that same technology they're immersed in every day. This book will show you how.

How do you capture the attention of the Connected Culture?

To understand and engage with the Connected Culture, it's important to first understand what they're most comfortable with…what they prefer. You've got to tap into their social network. Listen to their thoughts. Join in the conversation. Be a part of their world.

If words like "social media," "Google" and "texting" make you feel uncomfortable and confused, it's time to take some steps towards understanding the technology. But don't worry; you're in the right place. This book will easily define these subjects, explain their uses and describe how you can utilize this media to your advantage.

"IF YOUR TARGET AUDIENCE SPEAKS DIGITAL, SHOULDN'T YOUR ORGANIZATION SPEAK DIGITAL, TOO?"

— JERRY ALLOCCA

Does your organization really "speak" social media and search engines? To fuel growth and sustain a competitive advantage, you need to tap into the popular technologies and social networks that are now an everyday part of your customers' lives. These topics will also be covered in detail so that you can learn how to harness their power for your marketing advantage.

Learning to communicate with the Connected Culture

The Connected Culture is interactive. They seek out various means of interaction and form online connections with others. They are contributors as well as participants in social networks, blogs, forums and text messaging. Interactions are no longer limited to face-to-face contact or a telephone call. The Connected Culture uses digital technology to expand their world.

In order to effectively communicate with the Connected Culture, you need to speak their language. Let's explore the characteristics of their "speech:"

Responsiveness. The Connected Culture demands responsiveness. Today's technology driven generation is accustomed to instant gratification, and therefore expects responses in an instant.

Simplicity. The Connected Culture needs simplicity. Attention spans are decreasing—there's a premium on finding it fast and simple.

Openness. The Connected Culture is open. They are willing to share and display various aspects of their lives online.

Exploring your connections

This book explores all you need to know about connecting in the digital media world.

You will learn why we connect. You will pinpoint who you need to connect with and learn how you can make those digital connections happen. You will understand the tools of the trade and how they are used. Finally, you will be introduced to best practices and how other organizations are successfully using digital media to their marketing advantage.

Bonus! Download a free step-by-step guide for implementing the tools explored in each chapter.

Let's begin by thinking about why we connect...

SECTION ONE:
WHY WE CONNECT

Human beings are social creatures. We need interaction with other people. From childhood, we craved interaction, which—to our young minds—translated into attention. We wanted attention so badly we took it any way we could get it, good or bad. Good attention in the form of praise, compliments and advice. Bad attention like testing limits, mouthing off, getting yelled at for breaking something or doing something wrong. Getting attention was how we interacted with the adults around us.

What is one of the worst punishments you can think of in our culture? If you guessed isolation, you're right. Go directly to jail. Do not pass go. And definitely do not connect with other people. Isolating someone from the rest of society, taking away their ability to fully connect, is a punishment not taken lightly.

People connect because they need to feel like part of a group. To forge bonds and share common interests. To become involved and feel like an active, important part of the group. We want to express ourselves, and are emotionally rewarded when we share with a group that likes the same things as we do, where there is mutual passion.

There are good ways of connecting...

Making connections comes from a positive, natural energy. Some people genuinely like to make friends and brighten someone's day. Some like to help others. Some give advice. Some spread good karma. Some are a positive influence in the lives of others. Some teach and educate, or seek to heal.

There are bad ways of connecting...

Connections that are made unnaturally do not yield positive, healthy results. Some people try to sell you something for their own benefit, and don't particularly care if it benefits you or not. Some try to connect through deceit and hidden agendas. Some folks try to connect by complaining (misery loves company, as the saying goes). Some pass blame because they can't admit they could be wrong or they refuse to be accountable. Some are angry and want to spread the negativity. Connections made this way—or attempted to be made—go sour early.

And then, there's the BEST way of connecting...

Do you know what you want and how you want it? OK. Throw that out the window.

The best way of connecting, of reaching out, is to first seek to help. To find out what others want... and how you may be able to supply them with what they want and what they need.

Start out with an attitude of "I want to help," and you'll soon find the good connections flowing right back to you.

"SEEK FIRST TO HELP, THEN BE HELPED."

— JERRY ALLOCCA

CONNECTIONS ARE ESSENTIAL

Connecting with other people is an essential part of our existence. Connecting—in a good way—furthers our society and shapes who we are...and who we are becoming.

It is human instinct to be with others. People are gregarious, we are pack animals. We connect to get what we need, to help us live. Whatever we do or consume, we have the help of other people.

Still think you can get by without help from other people? Consider this. Take, for example, the fact that you are reading this book. Although you may be alone right now while reading, many different people helped you read this book.

For starters, someone taught you how to read. Someone paid for your education to learn about reading and comprehension. Someone wrote the words in this book. Someone edited the writing. Someone proofread the editor. Someone published the book and distributed it, and sold it to you. Someone shipped the book to you, and so on, and so on. This could go on forever, but don't ever think for a moment that you don't need other people or that other people aren't involved in everything that you do on a daily basis. It boggles the mind to think of all the different people that were involved in you being able to read this book. No matter what it is, you are always getting help from other people.

Connecting with people helps us get what we need, whether it's food, water, shelter, comfort, support, laughter—or this book. Connecting is essential to human existence.

21st century connecting

With today's internet, you can connect with a wider audience than ever before. The World Wide Web widens your circle by increasing the amount of people you can reach.

But considering the volume of people you can connect with today, can you really connect on a deeper, more intimate level? Does being connected to so many people water down the depths of your relationships?

Today, you can connect with groups of people on different levels. There are those select connections you will develop intimately; connections that you will water for growth. And there are those connections that simply help you feel...connected. Expanded, so to speak. Connections that help you express yourself, help you learn and get information, allow you to reach out to help others and receive help. Today, you can create different connections, on different levels, for business or for your everyday needs and personal life.

SECTION TWO:
WHO WE CONNECT WITH

A successful marketing campaign requires the development of positive, successful connections. Connecting with the right people— the audience who will pay for your product or service—can put you on the path to a winning campaign.

Choose your target audience

The first step is to describe your target audience in as much detail as possible. Really get inside their head. Who are you trying to reach? Who has the greatest need for what your organization does?

Take a look at your offering through the eyes of your audience.

• How will they benefit from using you?

_____

_____

_____

• What aspects of what you do is most important to them?

_____

_____

_____

• What are their greatest fears and concerns about your offering?

_____

_____

_____

_____

• What deciding factors make them choose one vendor over another?

_____

_____

_____

_____

• Is there an ideal gender? If so, which is it?

_____

_____

_____

_____

• Is there an ideal age range? If so, what is it?

_____

_____

_____

_____

• Is there an ideal geographic location? If so, where is it?

_____

_____

_____

_____

_____

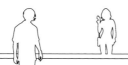

• Now really dig deep. What else can you write about your
  target audience?

_____

_____

_____

_____

_____

_____

_____

_____

_____

_____

_____

_____

_____

_____

_____

_____

_____

_____

_____

_____

_____

_____

_____

_____

_____

_____

SECTION THREE:
HOW WE CONNECT

So now that you know WHO you want to connect with, we can start exploring HOW you can reach out to your target market online.

Today, our interpersonal connections are expanded in ways that extend our reach to people all over the globe—in seconds.

Sure, people still connect the good old-fashioned (and still the most important) way—face to face. And we continue to connect via traditional media. But our reach has increased significantly via interactive media like cell phones, text messages, email, websites, chat rooms, discussion groups and now, social media—the media of conversations.

In this section, we'll explore the HOWs; the tools used to connect:

- Internet
- Websites
- Email
- Text Messaging and Mobile Marketing
- Search Engines
- Social Media

SECTION THREE:
PART 1: INTERNET

WHAT IS THE INTERNET?

The internet is a network of connected computers. That's right, apparently, even computers need to connect! But think about it. Most people think of the internet as some digital, cyber nonsense, a world of hardware, software and technology. But nothing could be further from the truth. What the internet really is, at its very essence, are networks of people. Behind every computer is a person looking to communicate in some way, shape or form.

Technical folks have connected together a network of computers —a "World Wide Web" of news and intelligence—so that they, and people in general, could communicate.

The internet's World Wide Web is evolving. Here is how...

Web 1.0

When the Web was first born and popular in the 90s, there was widespread computer illiteracy. There wasn't the computer in every home that you see today. Slow dial-up internet connections were the only way to connect your computer to the internet, and it worked through your telephone line.

Most importantly, content on websites were mostly static, read-only, a one way flow of information.

Web 2.0

Broadband or fast internet connections allowed you to view or load Web pages much faster, and you could finally watch videos.

Most importantly, content on websites became dynamic: a two way flow of information. Thanks to this interactivity, conversations can now take place. The Web went from being just a place to show online printed materials, to being a place to have highly engaging, interactive conversations with your customers.

The Web...in your pocket

Now you can take the Web with you. No longer are you limited to your computer at work or at home. Smart phones and other mobile devices enable you to search the internet or chat with someone 24/7, anywhere you are.

So where do websites fit in to all of this?

We'll explore that in the next chapter.

SECTION THREE:
PART 2: WEBSITES

WHAT IS A WEBSITE?

Simply put, a website is like your own broadcasting channel. It relates to a given topic. It contains sections and pages of information. Information can be broadcasted through words, pictures, sound, video, as well as through conversations. A website is like your own TV station, only it's not just a one way street. Yes, you can broadcast from a "one to many" perspective, but you can also invite one on one interaction. Your audience can respond to messages, news and media that you or others place on your website, and conversations, or transactions, can take place.

How do organizations use websites?

Like your frontline employees, websites work for you. They are engaging, 24/7 online representatives of your brand, product or service. Websites are also your virtual storefront. Your website should show off what value you have to offer; be a gathering place for customers and potential customers; a place where you can initiate feedback and promote conversations, and ask "how can I help you?"

Your website capabilities are limited only by your imagination, and your needs. Your organization may benefit from just a one-page, informational website, or you may be promoting a brand and services that benefit from many pages of sound, color, advertising and interactivity.

Is your website working well for your organization?

If you're like most marketing directors, you're always looking for ways to improve the results you get from your website. Measuring your website's performance reaps knowledge, improvement and rewards for your organization.

"YOU CAN'T IMPROVE WHAT YOU DON'T TEST."

— JERRY ALLOCCA

Websites: Testing for excellence

It's a good idea to perform a website self-test every few months to evaluate the quality of the online user experience for visitors to your site. Your reputation rests on it.

After all, the experience your user has on your website is similar to the experience a customer has with your employees on the phone or in person. It's vital that users have a positive experience.

Compare the strengths and weaknesses of your site to those of your competitors' sites. Your results will provide a greater understanding of what changes your site needs, which should translate into improved customer service and more qualified and productive leads.

How do you begin to analyze your site's strengths and weaknesses, and decide which improvements to make? You can perform a comprehensive, comparative assessment of your website based on these eight essential areas:

- First impression
- Navigation
- Branding
- Writing
- Design
- Visitor wait time
- Functionality
- Internet visibility

1. First impression

First impressions are lasting impressions. They set the stage for successful relationships. First impressions can be formed from a site's home page, a section's home page, or any page on your site—since you never know which page in your site a visitor will land on first.

Focus on answering these questions:

1. Does the first page a visitor sees on your website grab his or her attention at the get-go and motivate the user to learn more?

2. When you look at a competitor's website, what is your first impression of them?

3. Do you adequately differentiate yourself from your closest competitors?

4. Who makes the best first impression—you or your competitor? Why?

5. Is it clear what action the user should take next when they visit your website or are there too many choices?

When it comes to your website's first impression, communication is key. Clutter is a common mistake, since an overcrowded page confuses people and could cause them to leave. Give your most important desired action top billing and communicate clearly what is in it for the user—what value he or she will get. Decide what action you want visitors to take, and why it is in their best interest to do so.

2. Navigation

A site that's easy to navigate is a site that makes it easy for people to do business with you. Imagine that you are a new user to your site. Do you know exactly where to find what you are looking for? Ensure that information is provided quickly and intuitively. Make it as simple as possible by reducing the amount of clutter and organizing your information in a logical manner.

3. Branding

Advertising grabs their minds, but branding gets their hearts. The best brands strike an emotional chord and set you apart from your competition. What's more, strong branding projects credibility. Your brand is a factor in each page on your site. Make sure it brings out your uniqueness and gets your visitors to connect with your service or product.

4. Writing

Deliver your message clearly, communicate quickly and motivate the reader to take the desired action. Effective copywriting communicates its message with as few words as possible. Recent university studies show that the average consumer spends only two to three seconds deciphering the gist of a text passage, without reading the entire body of text. If you have too much copy, your audience may not absorb the information you are trying to convey. Make sure it is easy for visitors to understand what you have to offer, and let them see, quickly and effectively, why your services or products are the right choice.

Remember: Strong headlines draw them in, follow-through sub-headlines keep them reading and short but persuasive copy motivates them to action.

5. Graphic design

Visitors need a clean and professional image of your organization to take it seriously. The design should tell a story and reveal a more human, personal touch as selling almost always requires human interaction. Effective visual design highlights your good reputation.

6. Visitor wait time

Attention spans are decreasing, and your visitors will not wait long for a page to load. Pages that load fast have a clear advantage. If your site is graphics heavy, make sure those graphics are optimized for the quickest load-time possible. You can check your website's average load time at www.alexa.com.

7. Functionality

First, your site must work correctly and be coded properly. Make sure your code is W3C compliant. W3C (World Wide Web Consortium, www.w3.org), is an international organization that seeks Web interoperability. W3C develops standards, software and guidelines that ensure Web technologies are compatible with one another. Go to http://validator.w3.org and enter your URL to verify that your code is compliant with W3C standards.

The next step is to offer tools that your users can engage with. This will allow potential customers to read, chat about and interact with your brand with ease.

Web tools to consider for your site:
- Permission-based e-mail marketing
- Blogs
- Discussion groups / message boards
- Live chat
- Surveys and polls
- Social media integration

8. Internet visibility

Use alexa.com to see where your traffic rank falls. Then compare your rank to that of your competitors. Next, visit Google, Yahoo and Bing and test all your search terms. Take note of each competitor and what their current rankings are, and compare those rankings to yours. If your site isn't ranked high enough, then you have work to do.

Increasing visibility on the major search engines begins with keyword research. For proper optimization, develop a list of relevant, high-traffic keywords for each page in your website. Once a targeted keyword list is created, the site should incorporate several dozen search engine optimization (SEO) components that are necessary to increase rankings. SEO will be explained in an upcoming chapter, but simply put it's a way for searchers to find and choose your website over your competitors.

If you already have a keyword list, determine how each keyword is performing. Which keywords are getting you the best results, and which are just costing you money? Play up your winners and kill off your losers. You should always be testing and measuring new keywords.

There are two ways to increase visibility on search engines: on-page factors and off-page factors.

On-page factors include keyword mapping, keyword density, the implementation of optimized meta titles, descriptions and keywords, as well as paragraph headings or H1 & H2 tags in a keyword-friendly format.

Off-page factors include trusted inbound links, e-books, hub pages, your own blogs, other blogs, SEO article sites, social bookmarking, networking and other relevant social media sites.

These are just a few of the dozens of optimization factors that go into creating a high-ranking site on the major search engines. Initiation of link building programs and being actively involved with social media will further improve visibility and create more listings in the natural or free results area of Google, Yahoo and Bing for keywords that will drive prospective customers to your site. The chapter on search engines will elaborate on increasing your online visibility.

Websites: Next steps

Once you have played the role of visitor to your site and analyzed its strengths and weaknesses with an unbiased eye, you can determine where to go from there. You should also coordinate focus groups to get a truly unbiased opinion.

Planning and implementing a social media program is a good way to open up dialogs and drive traffic to your website.

The items mentioned in the Internet Visibility section are just a few of the dozens of optimization factors that go into making a site rank well on the major search engines. We recommend initiation of search engine optimization (SEO) and social media marketing (SMM) programs that will further improve visibility in the natural or free results area of Google, Yahoo and Bing. Search engine and social media programs will be elaborated on in other chapters of this book.

Website analytics should be in place so you can test and measure the performance of your site and make the proper adjustments to improve.

Overall your site should produce a positive experience for the user. It should grab their attention and allow users to find what they are looking for quickly and easily.

Your next step should be to create a strategic plan with blueprints. Decide on new goals and objectives, and create a plan for implementation. Be sure to roll out changes slowly to avoid disorienting frequent visitors. Your efforts will help your website receive the attention—and the sales—that it deserves.

Websites: Key takeaways

- ## First impression
  Is your website grabbing your visitors attention?

- ## Navigation
  Can visitors find the information they want quickly and easily?

- ## Branding
  Does your brand project credibility?

- ## Writing
  Is your content action oriented, and does it motivate users to some specific action?

- ## Graphic design
  Is your visual design clean and professional?

- ## Visitor wait time
  Are you making your visitors wait to get their information?

- ## Functionality
  Does your site do everything you need it to do?

- ## Internet visibility
  Are you found on major search engines when someone searches for what you do?

Websites: How do I get started?

Upgrading your website can be a daunting task without a plan. Take the time to determine your goals and what you want the website to do for your organization. The following workbook will show you how.

Download a step-by-step workbook for developing your website improvement plan.

SECTION THREE:
PART 3: EMAIL MARKETING

WHAT IS EMAIL MARKETING?

Email marketing is a form of direct marketing where you reach out to a large audience by using electronic mail— and have their permission to do so. One of the best ways to gain online exposure is using email marketing for special promotions, newsletters, invitations and information about products and services. When recipients open these electronic communications they can link to your web pages, driving more traffic and customers to your site. While individuals use email to keep in touch and communicate personal matters with others, organizations use emails to reach out to customers and solicit additional business while providing useful and interesting content.

The main objective of email marketing is to strengthen the relationship between organizations and their new and existing customers. And the fact that it's permission based means you're assured customers will be receptive to your message.

Thanks to internet technology, email is a versatile and commonly used form of communication. Industry giants like Google and Yahoo offer free email accounts for everyone. Emails can be delivered as simple text or as advanced web design techniques. Organizations need the more advanced email services in order to market their products and services to millions of people. The biggest advantage of email marketing is that the cost is very low when compared to other traditional mediums of advertising.

EMAIL MARKETING: THE BENEFITS

- Sell products or services
- Keep customers informed about your activities through newsletters
- Promote new product launches
- Maintain customer relations
- Announce special events
- Reach out to a large audience, even with a small advertising budget
- Increase revenue and expand your customer base while spending minimal marketing dollars

Building up trust

One advantage that stands out among email marketing's benefits is the opportunity to expand your organization's customer base. This is what ultimately translates into better sales and revenue. Loyal customers are likely to bring in repeat business as they become familiar with your messages and build up trust in your organization. With the amount of great advertising and marketing strategies employed today, it can be difficult for customers to build up more trust for one organization over another. This is where your email marketing can come to the rescue.

Cost efficiency

When designed and implemented correctly, email marketing has the potential to be one of the most effective marketing and sales tools. Besides, it is the most cost efficient way to promote special offers, discounts and announcements of new products or services to a large audience. Moreover, information can be distributed globally without any restrictions.

How do organizations utilize email marketing?

Sending an email to a customer requires much more than just hitting the 'send' button. The content of an email needs to be useful and motivate customers to purchase a product or service. What makes email marketing effective is not the sending of the message but the quality of copy. A well laid out email with images, audio or video clips can have a higher impact than just an ordinary email.

Email marketing vs. spam

Email marketing is not without controversy, as spam is a widespread and serious issue. It is important for email marketers to understand the finer aspects of email marketing and to know what spam and phishing is about in order to avoid it.

Spam is the use of electronic messaging systems to send unsolicited bulk messages indiscriminately. While the most widely recognized form of spam is email spam, the term is applied to similar abuses in other media as well.

Phishing is the criminally fraudulent process of attempting to acquire sensitive information such as usernames, passwords and credit card details by masquerading as a trustworthy entity in an electronic communication. Emails pretending to be from popular social websites, auction sites, online payment processors, banks or IT administrators are commonly used to lure the unsuspecting public. Phishing is typically carried out by email or instant messaging and often directs users to enter details at a fake website whose look and feel are almost identical to the legitimate one. However, there are stringent anti-spam laws that can lead to legal consequences for those who abuse email marketing.

Those that illegally purchase bulk email addresses through unscrupulous resellers or any other means can actually end up losers in an email marketing campaign. There are severe penalties that can be imposed by the Federal Trade Commission (FTC) in accordance with the CAN-SPAM Act (Controlling the Assault of Non-Solicited Pornography and Marketing Act). According to the Act, marketers are given 10 days to delete email addresses of individuals who opt out of their mailing lists. For this purpose, every email message must include the unsubscribe option.

Opt-in email advertising

It is important to understand various terms associated with email marketing. Emails are delivered to personal email boxes, which remains a sensitive issue, especially with the increase in spam. Opt-in email marketing is also known as permission marketing, where the recipient (the customer) agrees to receive emails.

Why do organizations use email marketing?

Many organizations focus their attention on email marketing as a medium to expand their customer base and build up a brand image. Moreover, they have realized the value of keeping in touch with their customers and most importantly they remain firm in their customers' minds. Organizations that fail to keep in contact with their customers succumb to the competition. That's because the customer has no choice but to choose a competitor who is more visible.

Selling products and services

Through email marketing, organizations are able to market their products and services more efficiently, resulting in better sales. A well planned marketing campaign with persuasive copy results in increased traffic to your site.

Generating repeat business

When your organization keeps in touch with customers through email marketing, it builds up brand loyalty with the potential to generate more sales.

Achieve business goals

Every organization has its own goals and a well planned email marketing campaign can help them achieve those goals. It creates opportunities to increase sales and revenue—the ultimate goal of any organization. With e-commerce booming, and more sites appearing online every day, competition gets tough. However, building up a brand image through email marketing will keep your organization ahead of your competition.

Keeping customers updated

Organizations use email marketing as a way to provide relevant information to customers about their products or services. This includes special offers, discounts, promotions, and the introduction of new products. This helps maintain a loyal customer base. For example, an accounting firm can use email marketing to keep customers informed about changes in tax laws or send reminders about filing their taxes on time. Clinics and hospitals use email marketing to inform patients about their checkups, reminders or modifications to the appointments and any other relevant information.

Saving on advertising and marketing costs

Undoubtedly, email is much cheaper than traditional forms of marketing with the potential to reach a wider target audience. Sending out appropriate email marketing messages helps retain customers. What's more, increasing the number of transactions per customer is much cheaper than acquiring new ones. The main elements of direct marketing, including frequency and timing of follow ups, are implemented in email marketing as well.

Measuring success

Email marketing has the power to measure the success of a campaign. Rather than guesswork, organizations can determine how many people have opened their email and what links they clicked. This type of assessment of campaign information is not available in other communication mediums.

Analyzing customer feedback

Since email marketing is highly measurable, organizations have the ability to analyze customer feedback and gather important leads on what customers are interested in.

Keeping up with the competition

With email marketing, smaller organizations have the perfect medium to keep up with their larger counterparts. Besides, it provides equal opportunities to large and small organizations due to its cost effectiveness. With e-commerce booming, more sales, more leads, and increased revenue is what email marketing helps organizations achieve.

CULTUREQUOTE»

"SPAMMING OR SUBSCRIBING PEOPLE WITHOUT THEIR PERMISSION HURTS YOUR REPUTATION"

EMAIL MARKETING: TOP CHOICES

Email marketing requires the assistance of an email marketing service. Desktop applications and internet service providers are inefficient when it comes to sending high volumes of emails to customers. Using an email marketing service ensures that email campaigns will not be considered spam, which is harmful for any business.

AWeber

AWeber is an automated email marketing software with tools to create, manage and build email lists to remain in touch with customers. Users can create unlimited campaigns to send out to prospective and existing customers in their opt-in lists. AWeber also provides a series of templates for those who do not have the writing skills for sales and marketing based letters. The service also includes a video tutorial for software installation and is backed by around-the-clock telephone support.

iContact

iContact is an easy-to-use email marketing software used for managing email campaigns. Some of the notable features include the ability to create and manage results from custom surveys and the auto responder that sends out automatic messages at pre-determined intervals. Included is a spam testing feature to ensure that emails do not land in a customer's spam box. Emails can be sent based on established demographics or filters. Most important are iContact's innovative campaign management and reporting features that are easy for first time users. Apart from video tutorials, the service also provides live support through email, phone and live chat.

Benchmark

Benchmark is among the most popular email marketing services that allows users to create compelling email campaigns and monitor results with ease. The service offers a comprehensive list of features which includes the ability to develop, deliver, and track bulk emails and manage campaigns. It also provides a large number of customizable templates. Benchmark includes an advanced email delivery to ensure that email messages are not spam. Additional features include the ability to create and send surveys, send video emails and free image hosting. Benchmark has a streamlined, easy-to-use interface, and includes a number of tools for marketers to build campaigns at their own pace. All this is backed by a variety of help options including a comprehensive FAQ and live support.

Campaigner

Another feature-rich email marketing service is Campaigner, from Protus IP Solutions. Included is a step-by-step wizard to guide users in creating a successful email marketing campaign. Other features include the ability to track the number of users that click on your links, import of emailing lists and HTML pages, and a contact list wizard. Campaigner offers several options to create customized reports that are essential for improving marketing campaign performance. An image editing tool to ensure that graphics fit within the design dimensions of a campaign is also an added feature that is rare among other services. Reports generated include emails sent, read, forwarded, bounced and unsubscribed.

MailChimp

MailChimp has an assortment of features with a simple interface that is easy to navigate. The service is popular with small as well as large organizations. Non-technical users will find tasks such as creating campaigns, managing subscribers, and generating reports easy to handle with drag-and-drop functions. Among the notable features are comparison reports to evaluate how campaigns perform against others, unlimited mailing lists and easy integration with Google Analytics.

Among the other email marketing services are Yola, Emma, Constant Contact, Vertical Response and more. The key is to enlist with a service that suits your specific marketing needs.

OK, so which one do I choose?

Choosing an email marketing platform depends on the priorities and preferences of an organization. While there are cheaper providers that offer services for little or no license fee, other services offer several additional features to maximize the effect of an email marketing campaign. However, some essential features should not be overlooked such as functionality, ease of use and customer support.

Features

It is important to evaluate the features of a platform prior to selecting one. Some email marketing platforms offer more flexibility than others. The key is to determine how useful these features are to your organization. A good platform will enable you to create and manage multiple campaigns and provide comprehensive reports. And most come with a free trial so you can evaluate it inside and out.

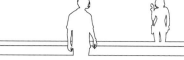

Ease of use

Most marketing professionals in organizations do not have the time to deal with technical details. It is advisable to choose an email marketing service that is easy to operate and can launch campaigns right away.

Templates

There are several email service providers that offer a large number of high quality templates. This saves plenty of time and money in creating messages and is an important feature to look for when choosing a service.

Email campaign creation and reporting

This is one of the most important aspects of email marketing. Make sure the service provides options to create different kinds of campaigns and allows campaigns to be customized, as well. In addition, a statistical representation of email campaigns is essential in order to compare the effectiveness of each one. The ideal email marketing service is one that provides ample campaign reporting options so that you are informed about a campaign's progress.

Help and Support

It is important to choose a provider that keeps its customers in mind by providing instant support via phone, email or live chat, preferably twenty four hours a day. The provider's website must also provide a comprehensive FAQ and troubleshooting section. Don't choose a service that scores less on customer support services.

The bottom line is to take a free trial or ask for a demonstration to help you make a decision. However, do not base your decision on the price. Most often, you get what you pay for.

EMAIL MARKETING: DO'S AND DON'TS

Email marketing can only prove effective when an organization takes the right approach. With stringent rules such as the CAN-SPAM Act in place, it is essential to adhere to guidelines set by the Federal Trade Commission. Below are some ways to make sure your campaign sets off on the right foot.

- **DO** make your email message unique to your organization's brand. Add a logo that is visible and a link to your website. Test all links before sending the message. This will leave a positive impression on your potential customers.

- **DON'T** engage in the creation of spam. Make sure people opt-in and include an opt-out option in accordance with the CAN-SPAM Act.

- **DO** consider using the services of an email service provider. These platforms are reliable and efficient ways to manage an email campaign.

- **DO** include a call to action in your email message. This calls for creative copy. Create a sense of urgency in the subject line, as well as at the top of the main message.

- **DON'T** write too much copy. Make sure that the copy is short and catchy with simple words and phrases. Bullet points improve readability significantly.

- **DON'T** forget to track the effectiveness of your messages on a regular basis.

- **DON'T** harvest email lists from harvesting programs on the web. This is considered illegal and unethical.

- **DO** create a snappy subject line that will raise curiosity and attract the reader's attention.

- **DO** plan your email marketing campaign well. Make sure you test it prior to launch. Many marketers make the mistake of rushing through with a campaign without proper thought to content, design, coding and, most importantly, metrics for measuring success of desired outcomes.

- **DO** review your email opt-in list periodically and before the launch of every campaign.

- **DON'T** send emails unless you have a specific message that is relevant. It takes less than a second for a customer to put you on the spam list.

- **DO** remember that email marketing is all about getting permission from customers and sending them relevant information they want to read.

- **DO** listen to the feedback from customers generated by reports provided by your email service provider.

- **DO** use your website's domain name as your email address.

- **DON'T** use email addresses from your personal gmail or yahoo accounts.

- **DON'T** make the mistake of ignoring campaign reports. This is the best way to measure results and make adjustments to your email marketing campaign. Check all the email statistics after every campaign ends and plan your improvements for the next one.

"ASKING FOR PERMISSION SHOWS RESPECT AND GUARANTEES AN INTERESTED AUDIENCE."

— JERRY ALLOCCA

EMAIL MARKETING: SUCCESS STORIES

History News Network (HNN)

Among the organizations to devote their efforts to email marketing is the History News Network (HNN), a Seattle based not-for-profit. The company's website HNN.com features the latest breaking news from a historical perspective with input from historians. A lot of the online magazine's content focuses on exposing historical misrepresentations by politicians. Earlier, HNN spent a small fortune to deliver email newsletters until they discovered the importance of an email marketing service to streamline their marketing campaign and improve its brand image. With the help of the Email Marketing Director from Arial Software, HNN introduced text as well as professional HTML newsletters, giving readers a choice of formats and easy opt-out as well. HNN now sends out three newsletters a week and has received a significant amount of website traffic (over 6,000,000 hits) and excellent readership response. In addition, they have managed to retain readers with over 13,000 subscribers to the HNN weekly newsletter. The website now receives around 300,000 unique visitors a month due to their email marketing campaigns.

American Precious Metals Exchange (APMEX)

APMEX is one of the companies to generate a significant return on investment through email marketing campaigns. Their first email marketing campaign with MailChimp generated over $157,000 in revenue, while spending less than a penny per email sent. The company was able to track the number of recipients that clicked over to their website, the number of customers that made purchases, and the amount of money they spent. This was possible due to integration of the email marketing service with Google Analytics. APMEX was able to launch a targeted campaign to suit their customer base. According to Marketing Director David McCarty, the company was able to cover their email marketing costs for the year with one single campaign.

CambridgeDiet.org

Weight loss and dieting is a competitive multi-billion dollar industry and small business owners like Pam Turner of CambridgeDiet.org need effective marketing campaigns to attract customers and retain existing ones. The website offers total health packages including a message board, personal dieting blog, and success stories. In addition, the website sells Cambridge Diet products. Initially, Ms. Turner's efforts at generating traffic focused on pay-per-click advertising. Ms. Turner expanded her marketing efforts to email marketing with AWeber. Her first opt-in email campaign involved an opt-in form in a prominent location near the top of the pages of the website. The second form was placed at the end of the home page for visitors to easily sign in. After signing up, customers are redirected to a webpage to confirm their subscription. On confirming their subscription, subscribers are sent to a custom page on the website where they can place an order, join a discussion group or read the FAQs on common Cambridge Diet questions. In addition, the website broadcasts a newsletter via the AWeber feed broadcaster. All Ms. Turner's blog posts are also delivered to subscribers through the email marketing system as a supplement. Due to the implementation of her email marketing campaign, the website has experienced a 300% increase in traffic with subscribers returning to the site. The messages sent have an average open rate of 47%, while the opt-in form has an opt-in rate of over 7%. Undoubtedly, sales have increased significantly and more people were made aware of the issue of obesity.

EMAIL MARKETING: INTEGRATION WITH OTHER MEDIA

Integrating email marketing with other social media platforms can increase customer loyalty and help marketers get the most out of online marketing. There is no doubt that email marketing and social media complement each other. Email newsletters can be shared and linked to social media platforms like Facebook and Twitter. Readers are also able to share messages and spread them to other social sites, thereby helping organizations build up a subscriber list.

Twitter and Facebook are among the most popular platforms used to integrate with email marketing. Email messages can include social media icons which create a direct link for the messages to be shared. This has the potential to increase click-through rates as much as 50% or more. Emails shared on social media sites like Twitter can increase click-through rates as much as 40% more than messages that are not linked to any social media.

Sharing links from email to Facebook

In many cases a large portion of an organization's subscriber list are already on social networking platforms like Facebook. Providing the tools to share in an email campaign helps readers to share content with the potential to lead to more subscribers.

To share a message on Facebook you need to use the "share URL" option created by Facebook.

For example: http://www.facebook.com/share.php?u=<url>

You will need to replace <url> with your link. This will create a preview of your content which can be posted to Facebook or sent as a direct message.

The key is to offer users a choice of platforms to share messages and align them with the mindset of customers engaging in social networks. This helps to build up a quality following and a potential customer base.

EMAIL MARKETING: KEY TAKEAWAYS

- Acquire permission
- Determine target audience
- Set up an email marketing platform
- Produce email
- Review opt-in list
- Test email
- Schedule and send email blasts
- Analyze campaign performance reports

EMAIL MARKETING: HOW DO I GET STARTED?

There are several factors to consider before entering the design phase. It is important to identify your marketing goals with an email marketing campaign and determine your desired results. The following email marketing workbook will help you get started.

Download a step-by-step workbook for developing your email marketing plan.

Download the Connected Culture Email Workbook FREE!

Visit: www.ConnectedCultureBook.com/freestuff

Enter in this code: email-workbook

SECTION THREE:
PART 4: TEXT MESSAGING AND MOBILE MARKETING

WHAT IS TEXT MESSAGING AND MOBILE MARKETING?

Wireless technology has brought about a unique approach to communications with mobile phones dominating the market. Mobile phones have become much more than person to person communication. Apart from sending and receiving simple text messages, an explosion of multimedia services available with mobile technology has caught the eye of many marketing professionals. High resolution color displays, video cameras, audio and video streaming, internet access, and multi-user 3D gaming are all common features of smart phones today. With texting becoming mainstream and multi-language options a common feature in mobile phones, organizations can utilize mobile phones to contact their target market easily.

Mobile marketing

Mobile marketing involves communication with potential consumers via mobile and other cellular devices such as smart phones organizations can send out marketing messages in the form of text messages to promote their products and services. This includes coupons and specials, running contests, or keeping customers updated on the latest in trends. Mobile marketing is one of the most cost effective marketing solutions available today. The affordability of mobile phones gives marketers the opportunity to reach out to the largest audience possible.

Text messaging and SMS

Text messaging is the cornerstone of mobile marketing. Commonly referred to as SMS, or short message service, an SMS is limited to 160 characters that can be sent to and from a mobile phone. Today, text messaging has become the primary mobile communications medium with over 2 billion text messages sent in a single day in the United States alone. From a marketing viewpoint, text messaging can be used to launch new products and services, offer voting services, trigger interactive calls, run contests and send text alerts. Even corporate giants such as Coca Cola launch targeted SMS campaigns and have started to move away from television advertising. SMS supports common short codes (CSC) where cell phone owners send replies to four to six digit short code numbers in response to advertising and marketing promotions. Texting is reliable, quick, easy to distribute and a cost effective way to launch marketing campaigns.

Text messaging and MMS

Multimedia Messaging Service (MMS) are messages that support graphics, audio and video. SMS and MMS are based on similar principles. However, MMS allows for audio and video attachments and web access to display content. Marketers can make use of these additional tools to maximize the effect of their marketing campaigns. Entry-level handsets are now available with MMS capabilities, making it easy to reach out to almost all demographics. For organizations, MMS can be used to launch viral campaigns. MMS messages concentrate more on the quality of content rather than character count. However, as compared to SMS, MMS is more expensive. MMS creates excellent branding opportunities for organizations where logos have a bigger impact, and image, video and other media rich content allow for better, more impactful branding.

Short code text messaging

Short codes are easy ways for potential subscribers to respond to campaigns. Short code instructions are usually advertised on billboards, radio and television. For example, for traffic updates you may be instructed to text "TRAFFIC" to 52525. Many organizations use their brand name as the short code. For example NIKE would be 6453. To launch mobile marketing campaigns with short codes you will need to use a text message service and contact your wireless provider.

TEXT MESSAGING: HOW SPECIFIC INDUSTRIES BENEFIT MOST

With billions of mobile phone subscribers worldwide, many organizations have begun to realize the potential of using text messaging and mobile marketing. An increasing number of organizations use text messaging as a way to communicate time sensitive and relevant information to their customers. These messages are sent instantaneously and can be read by the receivers at a time that is convenient to them. Text messages are received and read with a higher sense of urgency than emails, which is one of the biggest advantages of mobile marketing. According to statistics, an average of 94% of text messages are read by users. About 39% of consumers in the U.S. prefer to read text messages than listen to radio or TV ads when given a choice.

Education

Schools, colleges and universities communicate with parents and students by texting alerts and reminders. In addition, they use text messaging to inform prospective students about new courses, as well as emergency broadcasting of time sensitive events.

Healthcare

Hospitals, doctors and clinics use texting to send appointment confirmations and reminders to their patients. Texts are also a great way to keep patients informed of the latest developments in medicine.

Commercial establishments

Businesses use text messaging to send promotions and announcements to subscribers and build up their customer database.

Retailers

Apart from notifying customers about the status of their orders, retailers send coupons, exclusive offers and information about ongoing sales directly to mobile phones. In addition, they develop a database of customers who are interested in their products and services. Recipients of promotional offers can visit the retailer's store and redeem their offers right from their cell phones. Such messages can go viral with one customer distributing it to their family and friends, providing great exposure and the potential for the retailer to increase sales significantly.

Hospitality

Restaurants and hotels keep their customers informed about food and drink specials, special packages, discounts, complimentary admissions and reservation status through text messaging.

Real estate

Realtors text house hunters about property listings and use text messaging to set up appointments with prospective clients.

"WITH TEXT MESSAGING YOU CAN POTENTIALLY REACH MORE PEOPLE THAN THE INTERNET AND TV COMBINED."

— JERRY ALLOCCA

TEXT MESSAGING: TOP CHOICES

Organizations have a choice of text messaging platforms. In addition, each vendor offers a wide variety of services.

Mobivity

Mobivity is a user friendly and cost effective text messaging platform that includes many features for organizations to launch mobile marketing campaigns. These include SMS autoresponders, message forwarding, coupons, live interactive voting and the ability to manage contests. Most functions are accessible through the admin panel. Incoming messages can be forwarded to another mobile phone or email address. There are no contracts or sign up fees. The platform also offers a free trial with full access to the system.

MobileStorm

Apart from text messaging, MobileStorm offers email, voice and video promotions. The platform is ideal for clubs and restaurants with advanced features such as the RSVP Manager. Without paying a high monthly fee users can engage in a two-way interaction with their subscribers. The platform features auto-responders, scheduled messaging and a Carrier Queries function to determine which carriers belong to which numbers. MobileStorm also features a coupon management system with the ability to offer different discount types and choose the start and end date for the coupon. Another notable feature is the Text-to-Screen function, which enables voting results to be posted on video screens in real time.

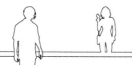

Texting Forward

Texting Forward is a text messaging platform with a number of exclusive features for launching mobile marketing campaigns. The platform has an easy to use campaign control center to create and monitor campaigns. It also includes a coupon redemption module to track coupon campaigns and build up a large customer database. The Reporting and Analytics module allows users to analyze the results of inbound and outbound offers in order to measure the effectiveness of particular campaigns. Other modules include voting, polling and surveys, and mobile loyalty programs.

PhindMe / EverywhereIGo

PhindMe combines text messaging with mobile site building services. Users can design, publish and host a website and then create and deploy text message campaigns, as well as register opt-ins. The platform offers a Mobile Marketing Association (MMA) compliant opt-in messaging system. It also enables users to capture leads, manage coupons and analyze campaign reports. There is a fully functional free version that can be accessed on a trial basis.

OK, SO WHICH ONE DO I CHOOSE?

Choosing the right text messaging service is an important task since each vendor offers a variety of capabilities. Here's what you should look for:

Easy setup

It is important to choose a text messaging service that is easy to install and hassle-free. The platform should either be web based or a desktop application that you can easily use to send messages to target groups. In addition, on a good platform you will not have to spend much time creating a campaign.

Ask for a demo

Many text messaging companies offer free trials. This will enable you to determine what works best to meet your organization's marketing goals. The provider should be able to demonstrate features and answer your specific questions.

Compatibility

The text messaging service should be able to deliver messages across protocols such as WAP, 3G, 4G and GPRS. These are the latest technologies available in handsets that are widely used. Any compatibility issues will result in your messages not being delivered and the potential to lose customers. In addition, the service must be able to deliver messages across all wireless carriers in order to increase the reach and effectiveness of your organization's mobile marketing campaign.

Bulk messaging

Marketing requires messages to reach out to as many customers as possible. The text messaging service should be able to send bulk SMS messages. This will help you reach a targeted group in a short time and generate more leads and customers.

Campaign management and reports

A good text messaging platform will allow you to create and launch campaigns with ease. Make sure you test this feature prior to choosing a service provider. It should also be able to generate comprehensive reports in order to determine the effectiveness of each campaign.

Look for a pilot partner

It is advisable to choose a vendor who can offer a long term partnership right from production to the launch of mobile marketing campaigns. Rather than simply sell their platform, the provider should offer total support in all aspects of SMS campaign management.

Branded SMS

It may make sense to choose a service that offers to brand your messages with your organization's name rather than a number in order to make a greater impact.

Expertise

Make sure you choose a provider that understands the various technology platforms as well as your organization's needs. A technology company that does not understand the finer aspects of mobile marketing can have an adverse effect on your marketing goals. A specialist will have expertise in best practices, short code provisioning and management, know how to grow databases, and also understand how SMS works with social networks.

Look for best practices

There are several rules and regulations when it comes to text messaging. Make sure the platform you use adheres to standards set by the CAN-SPAM Act including Mobile Marketing Association and Carrier guidelines.

TEXT MESSAGING: DO'S AND DON'TS

- When text messaging, **DON'T** use any jargon or 'lingo' that the recipient is not likely to understand.

- **DO** keep content brief and relevant and graphics to the minimum when using MMS.

- **DO** add a 'call to action' in your primary message.

- **DON'T** place a 'call to action' where it is not easily visible.

- **DO** integrate SMS with other forms of online and traditional marketing.

- **DO** allow customers to opt-out, and if they do, make sure you don't send messages to them.

- **DO** create an opt-in database and review the list periodically.

- **DO** review reports generated on a regular basis in order to determine the effectiveness of your mobile marketing campaigns.

- **DON'T** send messages without value. Sending messages too frequently, and without value, will annoy your subscribers.

- **DO** choose short and simple words that are easy to text.

- **DO** encourage customers to participate in contests and use a value-incentive to have them send responses.

- **DO** remove numbers for which you have received bounced or non-delivery messages.

- **DON'T** blend 'call to action' with other content. Make sure it stands out.

- **DO** use short codes and keywords, for example, text "ABC" to 52152, for running promotions and accepting responses to a competition or vote. It is advisable to use different keywords (like "XYZ") for each type of campaign in order to distinguish one promotion from another.

- **DO** run a smaller, pilot campaign and then move on to bigger campaigns. This will enable you to make adjustments to your marketing campaigns.

- **DON'T** repeat messages too often. Make sure you don't send the same content for two consecutive months.

- **DO** make sure to limit text messages to no more than 160 characters.

- **DON'T** use numbers as keywords. For example, (Text "25" to 52125 to get $25 off). Instead, use Text "DISCOUNT" to 52125 to get $25 off.

CULTUREQUOTE»

"DELIVER VALUE AND ACQUIRE PERMISSION"

TEXT MESSAGING: THE BENEFITS

Apart from being cost effective, there are many benefits to using text messaging and mobile marketing in an overall marketing strategy.

Quick and instant delivery

Text messages are received immediately, making it an ideal platform to distribute information quickly. This strategy works well for organizations offering discounts or special offers for a specific period.

Readability

A large percentage of text messages are read by subscribers as compared to other forms of media. Therefore, the chances of receiving responses are high. Moreover, since your messages are sent to those on your opt-in list, subscribers are most likely to take an active interest in your products or services.

Flexibility

Mobile marketing offers the flexibility to start campaigns whenever they are required, even on an urgent basis. For example, a retailer that wants to get rid of his stock before the end of the month can send out messages with deep discount offers.

Range of use

Mobile marketing can be used to promote a wide range of products and services. It is an easy way to announce product launches, one-day special offers, special events and more.

Building brand image

Mobile marketing offers organizations the opportunity to build their brand image. The viral nature of mobile marketing acts as a catalyst to spread the word to the largest possible audience.

TEXT MESSAGING: SUCCESS STORIES

Hyundai Auto Canada Corp.

Auto manufacturer, Hyundai, launched a mobile marketing campaign, "2009 Auto Show Circuit", with the objective of integrating mobile marketing and interactive brand management. Among their main aims was to build up a database of people who have interacted with the brand, generate leads for future marketing campaigns and analyze interactions in order to refine their marketing strategies. The company used prmText for text messaging, prmBlue for Bluetooth and prmTouch for a Touch Screen Kiosk. Attendees at the auto shows in various cities in Canada interacted with the Hyundai brand through multiple digital mediums. These mediums were used to enhance interest in specific Hyundai products and build up a customer database. Text messaging 'call to action' was featured on brochures, postcards and digital signage that were distributed by brand ambassadors to "Text HYUNDAI to 889988 to win 1 of 25 XM Satellite Radio Prize Packs." Text message participants received a WAP link, or link to a mobile website, to learn more about the company's line up of vehicles and forthcoming auto shows. iPod Touch units were used to capture information of qualified leads and enter participants into a grand prize contest. A special Bluetooth zone was included to create awareness of the brand where visitors received permission-based requests on their mobile phones as they passed through pre-set zones. The campaign enabled Hyundai to gather maximum consumer data and generate leads for their business.

McDonald's Canada

McDonald's Canada leveraged the power of mobile marketing in their "Open 24 Hours" to create an awareness of regional 24 Hours McDonald's Restaurants. Along with Cossette, an international communications firm, McDonald's launched a mobile marketing campaign where text promotion alerts were sent to subscribers informing them about 24 Hours McDonald's Restaurants. As part of the SMS promotion, participants were asked to respond to 1 of 7 keywords used on various media channels such as "Text 24 HOUR to 889988." Calls to action were displayed on radio, on signage in sports stadiums and at McDonald's outlets. The campaign was also promoted by McDonald's Street Team. Participants who responded were sent instruction to text message WIN daily to increase their chances of winning. Contest participants also received a text message every Friday announcing details of live in-store radio events. With thousands of text message entries and mobile participation during the live in-store radio events, McDonald's was able to reinforce their brand commitment and create a large customer database.

MGM Grand Casino

MGM Grand Casino successfully launched an SMS campaign powered by mobileStorm with prior permission from the conference organizers. About 300 guests attending the Prepaid Legal Conference were sent messages of special offers via SMS. More than 69% of the guests opted in and over their four-day stay received special offers on drinks at MGM's bars. Subscribers were allowed to forward the messages to their friends, making the campaign go viral. As a result, there were 549 redemptions of offers. In addition, the casino was able to boost their database and increase sales at their bars and restaurants as well.

TEXT MESSAGING: INTEGRATION WITH OTHER MEDIA

One of the main aspects that make mobile marketing a viable option is its easy integration with other forms of advertising and marketing media. The marketing success of an organization largely depends on its marketing mix. Mobile integration is possible by linking to other sites. For example, campaigns run from a .mobi site can include links to Facebook and Twitter accounts. It is also possible to create a mobile version of a blog so that it is accessible to readers through platforms like Blogger Mobile. Text messages are required to be compatible across all platforms including 3G and GPS.

Integration with social media sites provides unlimited promotional potential with mobile users being urged to participate through a 'call to action' and the ability to share information with friends via their social networks. This has the potential for a mobile marketing campaign to go viral. For example, a retail outlet can send out a promotional message that says, "Text TWORAYBANS to code 89898 to receive 30% off on Ray-Ban sunglasses today!" Those who respond can be provided a digital coupon to be redeemed at the store. Subscribers are likely to let their friends on Facebook and Twitter know about the offer, which in turn leads to better sales and revenue for the store.

TEXT MESSAGING: KEY TAKEAWAYS

- Acquire permission
- Determine target subscriber base
- Set up a text messaging platform
- Create promotional SMS campaigns
- Build your opt-in list
- Create your SMS message

- Broadcast your campaign
- Analyze campaign performance reports

TEXT MESSAGING: HOW DO I GET STARTED?

Text messaging and mobile marketing is easy as long as organizations make the effort to plan well. Through mobile marketing, organizations have the best chance to build the largest possible customer base and determine the success of a particular campaign. The following text messaging workbook will help you get started.

Download a step-by-step workbook for developing your text messaging marketing plan.

FREE STUFF!

Download the Connected Culture Text Messaging Workbook FREE!
Visit: www.ConnectedCultureBook.com/freestuff
Enter in this code: txt-workbook

SECTION THREE:
PART 5: SEARCH ENGINE MARKETING

WHAT IS SEARCH ENGINE MARKETING?

Search engine marketing (SEM) uses the everyday power of search engines (such as Google and Yahoo) to attract customers. Millions upon millions of people use search engines every single day to find what they are looking for. SEM helps them find your organization.

For the purposes of this book, SEM refers to search engine optimization (SEO) and paid search (PPC), also called pay-per-click. Although many trade associations consider only paid search advertising to be SEM, I believe that SEM includes search engine optimization, as well. Just as the term "marketing" is a big umbrella with many methods beneath its brim (such as advertising and public relations), SEM is also an umbrella that encompasses more than one method of marketing through search engines.

Many organizations have realized the value and importance of search engine marketing. It has enormous reach at just a fraction of traditional advertising and marketing costs. SEM has tremendous potential to increase sales, create brand awareness and maximize corporate visibility. In addition, SEM is effective in generating leads for an organization and building up a large customer base. The main objective of SEM is to drive prospective customers to your organization's website. This is possible through a combination of two techniques: search engine optimization (SEO) and paid search (Pay-Per-Click).

Search engine marketing concentrates your marketing efforts by increasing traffic (the number of visitors) to your website from search engines. Most importantly, it aims to boost your conversion rate which is the percentage of visitors who become customers. Traffic to your site is increased by upping your search engine visibility; that is, the position of your website in the search engine results generated by specific keywords that web users type into the search box. If a site appears on the first page of the search results, it is more likely that such visibility will bring a high volume of web visitors.

Objectives of SEM

The main objectives of search engine marketing are to:

1. Improve website visibility for acquiring maximum traffic.
2. Improve the quality of traffic based on selected keywords that appeal to visitors, resulting in a conversion.
3. Decrease expenses by eliminating underperforming keywords.

In order to master both SEO and paid search, your organization will need to spend a considerable amount of time on both strategies. That's because the marketing dynamics keep evolving every few years or so. It is also important to keep abreast of changing trends in order to achieve and maintain a high rank in the search engines.

Search engine optimization (SEO) – natural search

Search engine optimization (SEO) is also known as natural search placement. "Natural" because your organization can incorporate SEO strategy without having to pay to be listed and ranked high on search engines. SEO strategy entails optimizing a website—enriching its content in a very specific way—in order for the site to be noticed by search engines and by targeted visitors. This optimization involves the use of keywords and key phrases – popular search terms used by people when searching for products or services on the internet. SEO strategies also include submitting your website to directories and link building.

Aiming for one of the top ten positions in Google is not the only benefit of SEO. SEO also helps an organization analyze the competition, monitor traffic and, finally, convert traffic into leads or sales.

Sites that are well optimized can make it to the first few pages of major search engines, enabling a website to gain better online visibility and generate free leads. SEO is efficient and cost effective, but it needs consistent upgrading and monitoring in order to maintain and continually improve your site's search engine ranking. Results will be seen, but not instantly, as it takes a special expertise to remain search engine friendly, including constant monitoring and modifications to underperforming pages on your website.

Important factors of natural search

Natural (organic) search results are gathered by search engines and ranked according to relevant keywords that are assessed by a specific algorithm. Unlike paid search results, they do not require any fee since they are indexed by search engines based on matching keywords.

- Search engines index web pages based on algorithms or complex formulas.
- Websites are not required to pay for listings
- Most cost effective search engine marketing technique
- Has the potential to drive far more traffic than paid search
- Natural search results are not as predictable as paid search results

Pay-per-click (PPC) – paid search

Paid search is commonly referred to as PPC, or pay-per-click. PPC enables organizations to legally purchase top positions in search engines with small ads on the right-hand side of the search engine results page and in some instances at the top of the search engine results page. These ads are an instant way of reaching out to customers, making paid search an effective way to increase the visibility of an organization's website in search and directories. Its rapid increase in popularity in recent years is an indicator that it has great potential for organizations of all sizes.

PPC involves a bidding process. This may sound like an expensive option, but organizations who are able to stretch their budget in an attempt to gain online exposure will quickly find this a viable marketing strategy. First, you need to determine keywords that customers are likely to type into a search engine to locate your website. If your bid for your chosen keyword is the highest, and your ads perform well, you have the chance of obtaining instant exposure as your advertisement will be displayed in the top positions. Each time a user clicks a link on your ad, you are required to pay the search engine (hence the phrase pay-per-click). On platforms like Google AdWords, competitive keywords attract high bids for keywords relevant to a target audience.

Important factors of paid search

Some factors that make paid search different:

- A bidding system is used to pay for each click on your listing, but no fee is charged if nobody clicks on your listing
- They tend to produce quicker results and can be implemented faster
- Bids can be high, leading to increased costs

SEO (NATURAL SEARCH) OR PPC (PAID SEARCH): WHICH ONE SHOULD YOU CHOOSE?

If you want the potential to reach 100% of people searching on search engines, you need to employ a mixture of both SEO and PPC.

It is important to note that research indicates that 84% of Google users do not go past the first page of natural search results. This is a clear indication that every attempt must be made by organizations to maximize their SEO efforts so they appear within that first page. Marketers must also be aware that about 65% of Google users ignore paid search listings since they find organic search results more relevant than PPC. These users tend to have a higher level of education and tend to conduct very specific searches.

The bottom line is to select keywords carefully and adopt the right link building strategies in order to reach the top rankings in search engine result pages. There are no costs involved in organic search results. However, it will take time and effort to determine the right SEO strategies that need to be combined in order to produce higher rankings. It requires careful planning in order to implement effective web marketing strategies.

SEARCH ENGINES: TOP CHOICES

Marketing directors have a choice of paid search platforms to help them launch online marketing campaigns. Popular search engine sites include Google, Yahoo, Bing and more. Each site has its own method of indexing web pages and offers its own style of paid advertising programs.

GOOGLE ADWORDS

Organizations have the potential to target customers at the very moment they search for products or services relevant to their industry. To boost this marketing power, Google developed AdWords. AdWords are text ads that appear as 'sponsored links' on a Google search page in response to searches for certain keyword phrases. Google AdWords is based on the pay-per-click system. You are required to bid for a series of phrases in order to have an ad appear on the search page. However, you need to pay the amount of the bid if someone clicks on your ad. The ad includes a title line, two lines for a short description and a URL to your web page or landing page. The higher your bid, the higher your ad can be placed on the search pages. Research indicates that about 84% of users do not go past the first page. Therefore, it would be advisable to bid for ads that give you the highest possible visibility.

Google AdWords is an ideal way to target specific customers. Searchers who are looking for a particular product or service are more likely to click on your ad if it relates directly to their search. However, it is essential to manage these PPC campaigns effectively. If visitors do not find what they are looking for on your website, it would simply be a waste of your marketing dollars. Marketers must be aware that Google also offers CPC or cost-per-click, CPM or cost-per-thousand impressions, and CPA or cost-per-action options. The main feature of these options is that text ads can be displayed on third-party sites. This enables advertisers to reach out to a larger audience on other sites in addition to Google. About one third of Google's revenue comes from these programs.

YAHOO! SEARCH MARKETING

Yahoo! Search Marketing offers organizations the opportunity to connect with customers who are looking for products or services they sell. Yahoo offers various options that include local advertising, sponsored search, search submit, travel submit and more. Ads appear in Yahoo's search engine results as well as across other search engines.

The additional features on Yahoo Search Marketing include keyword research tools, ad testing, geo-targeting, forecasting and more. Geo-targeting allows you to place ads by country, state, city, zip code or DMA (Designated Market Area). Content Match is another way organizations can reach out to customers through emails and newsletters. Ads that are placed will appear not only within the search rankings, but also next to relevant articles and product reviews.

The Yahoo! Sponsored Search option allows users to create ads that appear in its search engine results as well as other sites on the Yahoo network. This enables organizations to target specific audiences across a large market. Yahoo supplies a number of tools in order to manage search marketing campaigns effectively.

Once you set up an account you can target customers according to their geographic location. The next step is to choose relevant keywords, determine the amount you want to spend and then create an ad which can be displayed within minutes of it being approved by Yahoo administration. You are charged every time your ad is clicked on for the amount you agree to pay. Yahoo also offers the Yahoo Directory where organizations can list their names for free. Alternatively, users can pay for a featured listing.

Yahoo Sponsored Search also offers the option of targeting prospects that search for products or services within your local neighborhood.

For beginners, Yahoo! Search Marketing offers tutorials and support in addition to tools for managing PPC campaigns. These include the Keyword Selector Tool, View Bids Tool, and PPC ROI Calculator. For those willing to invest, Yahoo! Search Marketing could be an ideal tool to use as part of an online marketing campaign.

Bing and Yahoo

The recent Bing and Yahoo alliance is set to capture a significant share of the PPC search market. In a recent agreement, Bing powers Yahoo's search engine results. Since paid-search ad spending rose 5.8 percent in the third quarter of 2010, advertisers can look forward to positive results in their PPC campaigns. These campaigns cost less than Google AdWords. However, Google has the highest exposure and currently leads in PPC advertising. One of the main advantages of Bing PPC is that you can target specific markets according to age and gender. You can increase your bid by different percentages. For example, you can increase your bid by 10% for the age group of 35-45 and by 20% for women. However, Bing will only be able to identify customers that log in through their Windows Live accounts.

Advertising on social networks

Social media sites such as Facebook, Twitter, MySpace, and YouTube have advertising and marketing options for organizations to explore within the framework of social media. Although basic social media in the form of instant messaging and forums have been around for a while, the Web 2.0 movement and the introduction of powerful social media sites have changed the way online marketing campaigns are conducted.

Social media sites such as Facebook and LinkedIn allow organizations to gain online exposure when using these social networks for marketing strategies. According to estimates by eMarketer, social networks are likely to bring in over $3 billion in advertising revenue in 2010, which is an increase of $2.5 billion from 2009. Facebook is likely to gain $1.3 billion of that share.

It is important not to simply apply the same rules of advertising to all social media sites. Each one has its own unique features that can prove effective when combined with other media sites. Social media campaigns do not tend to work in the same way as search marketing campaigns.

Facebook has various pay-per-click advertising options including CPM (cost per thousand impressions) and CPC (cost per click) models. The Facebook Ads Manager is a simple tool designed to enable organizations to target specific markets since Facebook holds all their profile information and will only display your ad to those that match your criteria.

SEARCH ENGINES: THE BENEFITS

Effective SEO campaigns are cost effective ways of implementing marketing strategies with the minimum amount of capital. These campaigns have the potential to bring a higher return on investment than any other form of marketing thereby increasing overall sales and profit. Websites that are well optimized increase their chances of being picked up by search engines and ranked high. An increasing amount of visitors to a website also enhances the exposure that an organization's products and services receive globally.

In order to maximize SEO results, it is important to select the right key-words and key phrases. Your web content must contain keywords relevant to your business and should be popular terms used by people on search engines. It is important to keep changing keywords and phrases according to their popularity. However, care must be taken not to stuff a page with too many keywords.

Paid search vs. natural search: The statistics

Search engines like Google serve more than 60 million unique visitors each month and gets over 76 billion searches per month. These figures increase at a rapid rate, which indicates that the online environment is firmly entrenched as a media of choice for consumers. According to statistics, 41% of individuals use search engines to search for information on products or services they desire. This presents the ideal opportunity for organizations to include search engine marketing as a major part of any online marketing initiative.

Google's "golden triangle"

In a study conducted a few years ago, users were tracked to see what their eyes focused on when browsing through search engine results. Studies indicated that users' eyes scan a search page in a triangular track that includes moves from the top sponsored and top organic results, down to Google's alternative results, along with shopping, news and local suggestions. Visibility of the top fold was 100%, and dropped to 85% for the bottom listing in the 'above the fold' section. Visibility dropped further below the fold from 50% at the top to 20% at the bottom.

CULTUREQUOTE»

"BECOME A VALUABLE INFORMATION RESOURCE"

SEARCH ENGINES: DO'S AND DON'TS

For natural search listings (SEO):

Search engine optimization requires constant monitoring and changes to be implemented in order to make it to the top of search engine rankings. Therefore, a few factors need to be considered prior to implementing an SEO campaign. There are no hard and fast rules in SEO that can guarantee top rankings. However, here are a few guidelines to take into account:

- **DO** conduct a keyword analysis regularly. You cannot optimize your website without prior knowledge of keywords that are popular. It is important to use keywords relevant to current search engine trends, which must be reviewed and changed periodically.

- **DON'T** use too many keywords on a page. Keyword stuffing is considered cheating by search engines. Maintain a keyword density that is also appealing to the reader (3-5 out of every 100 words).

- **DO** update the content on your website regularly. Search engines are not likely to notice web pages that lie dormant for weeks. Besides, updated content lends credibility to a website and greater interest for your visitors.

- **DON'T** hide keywords in comments or in code where they do not appear on-page to the user. This is called cloaking, and you will get caught.

- **DO** use filenames relevant to keywords for every web page.

For example, if the page is about dog toys the file name can be yourdomain.com/dogtoys.html.

- **DON'T** have a series of irrelevant sites linking to each other in an attempt to fool spiders with false link popularity. This is called link farming, and search engines don't like it. You will get caught.

- **DON'T** optimize for keywords to pull in searchers, but then direct them somewhere else that is not relevant. This is called a gateway page and is another form of SEO cheating.

For paid search listings (PPC):

- **DO** make sure your ad copy uses relevant keywords. It should contain the main keyword so that it is displayed in bold in search results.

- **DON'T** use the same ad copy over and over in PPC. Create ad groups and test different ads and see how they perform. Ad copy must be reviewed and changed from time to time. Lowest performing ads must be reworked in order to maximize the click through ratio so constant improvement is necessary.

- **DO** make sure to check the guidelines and restrictions of PPC campaigns. In addition, it is important to monitor the performance of your campaign to get the best return on your ad spend.

- **DON'T** leave your campaign on auto-pilot. Check your results often and refresh content whenever you can.

- **DO** monitor your campaign constantly and always seek new ways to improve every aspect of the campaign's performance.

SEARCH ENGINES: HOW TO IMPROVE YOUR RANKINGS

Search engines rank web pages based on algorithms or complex formulas.

Each major search engine—Google, Yahoo, Bing and the like—has its own "top secret" algorithm. Although they are all unique, these algorithms do have some important aspects in common:

Commonalities in the ranking formula:

- Location (Title, Description, META, headline, body copy, alt tags)
- Frequency (no more than 5 out of every 100 words)
- Link Popularity (what sites are referring you?)
- Inclusion in other indexes and directories
- Site design / structure / spider-ability

How can you improve your rankings within each formula?

- Become a valuable information resource
- Proper keyword research
- Website optimization and properly coded web pages
- Link popularity and ongoing link building programs
- Regularly create valuable content
- Avoid being blacklisted from search engines
- Use XML sitemaps
- Submit your site
- Test and measure

"YOU CAN'T IMPROVE WHAT YOU DON'T TEST"

— JERRY ALLOCCA

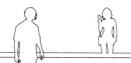

Test and measure

You can't improve what you don't test. Reliable analytics must be in place along with a process for generating reports and analyzing the results. Test the response you get from each ad and lead source. How many conversions? What was the cost per conversion? Make adjustments to the lower performing ad, then test again and compare with past results. Stick to what works, until it stops working.

Keyword research

When used properly, keywords build the very foundation of a successful search engine friendly website. Implement keywords within each unique page in your site. But don't overdo it. You want the keyword to fit comfortably and flow naturally within your site.

When researching keywords, find out what the estimated monthly searches for each search term are—on each major search engine. Sites like Wordtracker and Keyword Discovery are excellent tools for finding out what the best keywords to use are, as well as what the competition is using. Discovering what keywords "the other guy" is using is important. A popular keyword will be used so often that it may not improve your ranking at all. Very often, using more specific 3-, 4- and 5-word search phrases are easier to win. You'll want to use phrases and words that are searched enough to pull in customers, but not so competitive that your site will get lost in a sea of other web pages rich with the same keywords you are utilizing.

Properly coded web pages

The best architects build a house to stand the test of time, using well-thought out blueprints and strong foundation materials. Your website should be built, or "coded," the very same way.

META tags are a vital website building block, and provide crawlers with information about the content of your site's web pages. When the language in which web copy is written for your META tag is properly coded, it should contain a relevant title, description and keywords. Good META tags make your web pages easier to find and help searchers choose your listing over your competitors.

When coding web pages, ensure that you use keywords in headline tags (H1, H2). Furthermore, keyword use at a formulated rate in the web page copy is of vital importance.

The relationship between content and keywords is key. To rise in the ranks of search engines, optimize your site by building content around your most important keywords.

Embedding a keyword within your URL can also aid in your site's higher ranking. For example, www.businessschool.edu will make the marketing and visibility of this organization's website more relevant on the major search engines for the keyword "business school."

Once you have established successful keywords, use keyword mapping to strategically link these words to specific pages of your website.

Finally, use the proper density for your keywords. Use them too much, or "stuff" them into your pages, and you may get blacklisted. The optimal density for keywords within your web pages is 3-5 out of every 100 words.

Link popularity

Link popularity is a score that measures the number of external web links that link directly to your organizations website. Link popularity is a large part of every major search engine's current algorithms. It is a very important ranking factor. So...how do you get "popular?"

First of all, pay close attention to who is referring you. Link popularity takes the quality and importance of the links into account. For example, this means that linking to a major business directly related to your industry will help your site's ranking. Do not link to an irrelevant business or website like someone's personal homepage. Do the proper research on gaining trusted inbound links and look to link with sites that are naturally related to your own industry.

The higher your site's link popularity, the more your website is seen as relevant, helpful and worth presenting. Most important, it becomes highly referable!

Ongoing link building programs
- Directory listings
- Reciprocal linking
- Blogs / Forums / RSS feeds
- Social media sites
- YouTube search engine optimized videos
- Article and press release submission sites

Convince them to click on *your* link

There is a lot of competition on a search engine results page. The most clicked on listings usually have a unique value proposition that makes them the clear choice over their competitors. The listing communicates its uniqueness and attracts a certain market.

You have to promise them something of value, and deliver on your promise. You must write qualifying, descriptive copy and encourage those you want, and discourage those you don't.

You must have a clear call to action which motivates your audience to take the next step so your organization will achieve its desired result.

SEARCH ENGINES: KEY TAKEAWAYS FOR SEO

- Determine marketing goals
- Analyze the competition
- Create good content
- Prioritize web pages
- Optimize web pages
- Fine tuning your plan
- Combine natural search with PPC

SEARCH ENGINES: KEY TAKEAWAYS FOR PPC

- Target your customers
- Create your ad groups and ads
- Set pricing
- Launch campaign, then measure and tweak

SEARCH ENGINES: HOW DO I GET STARTED?

As a marketer, one of your main objectives is to drive traffic to your website. Therefore, it is essential to develop a search engine marketing plan to use as a reference when you run your campaign.

Download your step-by-step workbook for developing your own search engine marketing plan.

Download the Connected Culture Search Engine Workbook FREE!

Visit: www.ConnectedCultureBook.com/freestuff

Enter in this code: sem-workbook

SECTION THREE:
PART 6: SOCIAL MEDIA

WHAT IS SOCIAL MEDIA?

Social media is communities of people having conversations online.

Social media is websites and tools for sharing and discussing information. One thing that differentiates social media from other forms of media is that it is a user-based construction of media. This means you create the media. You create the words, pictures, videos and audio. You create the message—not the TV stations, or the radio stations, or the newspaper publishers. The control is now in your hands.

Time and money

The amount of time and money put into traditional media and social media are what sets these methods apart. With traditional media, it costs a lot of money, but very little time to run your ad. All you have to do is pick up the phone and "reorder" another flight on TV, or more space in the newspaper. Once your ad or commercial is created, it takes very little time to continue advertising.

With social media, the cost is very low, or free in some cases. But you have to spend a lot of time. And whether you spend the time yourself, have an employee spend the time, or outsource to someone else to spend the time, time is the key.

Social media is easy to use, but it's how you use the technology that matters. I hear people say, "just hire a kid to do your social media marketing". And while "a kid" may be able to use the technology, what do they really know about how to market your organization or sell your products and services? Social media marketing requires a very soft sell, great curiosity-based questions and the creation of value for your audience. Would you really trust a kid to do all that? Remember your reputation is at stake. Don't leave your reputation in the hands of just anybody.

Schedule time in your calendar for social media

Maintaining a schedule is a vital part of keeping our day to day lives organized and on track. Throughout our days we schedule meetings, phone calls and lunch appointments. If you are trying to increase business for your organization or communicate with the Connected Culture, add social media participation into your schedule, too.

When I say add social media to your schedule, I don't mean make time to play Farmville with your friends on Facebook. Make time to have meaningful conversations with your business peers on social media sites like LinkedIn, Facebook and Twitter. LinkedIn provides an online networking meeting place, and just like face to face meetings, you should schedule time in your day to meet online with other business professionals. Let's face it, nobody ever has time, but you make time for things that are important to you. Make the time to connect with other business professionals and continue your networking after the face to face events are over.

I've found that if you don't put something in your calendar, it usually doesn't get done. Adding social media time to your schedule is the best way to ensure that you make time to get noticed. The great thing about social media is that there are no time restrictions. You can participate when it is convenient for you. Plan your social media time around your schedule. It doesn't have to be a huge block of time, but you do need to plan it into your day. Plan it for 30 minutes of your lunch hour. Or perhaps instead of watching that show on TV at night, you could have an online conversation. When you commit the time, you will build relationships. Start planning this time now.

Social media is social interaction and that takes time. It comes in many different flavors, including blogging, microblogging, networking, videos, photos, news and bookmarking. These mediums are all designed to encourage discussion and communication, and will be discussed in detail in the following sections.

WHAT IS SOCIAL NETWORKING?

The 21st century brought with it several powerful "connection" solutions through technology, including social networking—the revolutionary medium through which most of the world communicates today. Simply put, social networking is having conversations online and sharing information with the hope of growing relationships, creating value and nurturing win-win situations.

Whether it is for personal or business needs, social networking is the most popular means of online communication. Apart from developing friendships and professional contacts, social networking is used for finding employment and marketing your organization, as well. All of this is possible through websites that serve as social networking platforms. These include Facebook, LinkedIn, MySpace and many more.

Marketing opportunities

Social networking offers organizations like yours an array of marketing opportunities. The key is to learn to use these platforms efficiently. Although it may not be an effective marketing tool on its own, it can be used to complement other marketing strategies. Integrating social networking with other marketing strategies can boost your organization's marketing efforts and produce measurable results. Better yet, these platforms can help to build a global business with minimal overhead costs.

Low-cost marketing platforms

Social networking platforms are great budget-savings tools, allowing organizations to expand their markets significantly by building up a Web presence without spending a lot of marketing dollars. The main advantage? Reaching out to a niche market in any time zone at a fraction of the cost of traditional marketing. It doesn't matter whether you are a small business owner, large organization, a musician or a journalist—social networking is a good way for people to get to know you and learn more about your products or services. However, the key to success is to interact regularly and provide valuable information or help, since that is what people look for on the Web. In addition, it is important to understand which groups of users you should reach out to for success.

Leveraging the power of networking

There are two main ways to leverage social networking sites for marketing purposes: purchase advertising slots, or start a viral campaign. Going viral is possible because people can post and share information with millions across the world, almost in an instant. Social networking sites allow users to quickly "spread the word" to others, including friends, relatives and business colleagues. Information is exchanged rapidly across networks and circles of influence.

Creating brand awareness

One of the advantages that marketing directors can derive from social networking sites is the ability to generate a buzz about their products or services and increase brand awareness. What's more, most of the popular social networking sites are free, which is ideal for marketing on a tight budget. But you do have to spend time, or hire the right person to spend time making social networking work for you.

Pay-per-click advertising

For the long term, the value for marketing on social networking sites may be simply the ability to reach niche groups via advertising. Most of these sites have targeted text advertising with fees in reach of small businesses. LinkedIn's fees can be as low as $5 for 1,000 impressions, and LinkedIn also allows users to set a budget. Advertisers can choose to target several criteria, which include geography, industry, seniority and company size.

Prior to launching any marketing campaign on social networking sites, it is essential for your organization to understand the need to remain consistent and committed in the long term. The key to success is to select appropriate social networking sites that align with your organization's marketing goals.

SOCIAL NETWORKING: TOP CHOICES

The rapid growth of social networking sites has made marketing directors sit up and take notice. Sites such as Facebook and LinkedIn have fueled much excitement and speculation among professionals in the business community. To make the most of these sites as a marketing tool, you need to be aware of what types of social networking sites exist and then use a few that suit your organization's needs.

Facebook

Look through any research on social networking and Facebook always seems to come out on top. Though the website was initially meant for college students, it has grown far beyond that. With the largest number of members by a big margin, Facebook offers organizations the best possible shot at marketing, since there is the potential for reaching far more people. The site has an option for creating a business account and a business fan page to administer ad campaigns. However, for greater reach it is advisable to open a personal account, as well. Since Facebook is more of a general social networking platform with diverse niche groups and communities, organizations can take advantage of its reach by asking users to join them on Facebook, rather than asking these people to remember their organization's URL from a television or print ad. And the advantages are numerous: Facebook encompasses many other functions, such as blogging and discussion groups, microblogging, sharing and commenting on photos and videos, and much more.

LinkedIn

LinkedIn is a social networking site for business professionals. It allows organizations and their employees to reach a very large network of business professionals. The site allows users to participate in discussion groups and question-and-answer forums based on niche topics. LinkedIn allows you to communicate directly with people you want to contact. In addition, members can search for you. This gives business professionals and organizations the opportunity to build relationships and new contacts while marketing themselves. LinkedIn serves almost every industry and profession. One unique feature of the site is that members can use it effectively for sales and marketing, as well as for human resources.

MySpace

Another powerful social networking site where organizations can market their products and services is MySpace. The site attracts the second largest number of new users per day, especially since News Corp. acquired it for $580 million back in 2005, only two years after its launch. It serves as an ideal platform through which to form ties with other professionals and promote products and services in a personal environment without any loud marketing tactics. The website allows you to create blogs, which is a good way to provide information that is valuable to your audience. Blogs are ideal for creating links back to your website and can be used to spread information related to your products or services. However, you need to make sure to remain an active member and keep information up-to-date. In addition, be honest and be friendly, which are two essentials in order to convert members into lifelong customers.

Meetup.com

Meetup is a niche social networking website for local in-person groups. You coordinate details online such as the meeting place, event info and how to register. You attract people based on your niche, your mutual interest and your location. It allows local groups to coordinate activities online while they meet face to face.

Twitter

Twitter tops the list in microblogging—a form of networking and communicating through short blogs or messages of 140 characters or less. "Tweets" (the name given to posts on Twitter) present organizations the opportunity to inform members of new blog posts, special deals, contests—anything of interest. Twitter is a simple yet powerful tool to connect with large groups, making it an attractive option for marketers to reach their target market.

There are plenty of other social networking sites that you can test according to your business' niche. On the upside, whatever your organization is all about, you are most likely to find a specialized network for it.

OK, SO WHICH ONE DO I CHOOSE?

While there are various sites being used successfully by organizations in a bid to increase awareness about their products or services, it is essential to experiment with a few networks suited to your specific type of organization. Once you evaluate these sites, it is easy to determine which ones would work best to benefit your marketing campaign.

Site popularity

Social networking sites like Facebook and LinkedIn have a large number of members, which enable you to reach out to more people with the least amount of effort. It makes sense to experiment with sites that are popular. You can be sure the biggest players will still be around in the next few years, and will give you the potential to reach far more people.

Features

Depending on the type of products or services you need to market, it would be prudent to choose sites that offer an abundance of features. Before selecting a social networking site, make a list of what your criteria and goals are and compare similar sites that are a match. For example, if you need to drive traffic to your blog, then you should consider Twitter, since it allows you to link to your blog post. For networking with business professionals in your industry, LinkedIn may be more effective.

Mere numbers don't count

It is important to choose social networking sites not for the number of members but rather for the total number of active members. Moreover, these members must fall within your target audience. A site with a big list of inactive members won't do your marketing strategy any good.

"CREATE VALUE, NOT SPAM."

— JERRY ALLOCCA

Site policies

Since marketing involves plenty of promotion, it is essential to understand a site's policies on using it as a promotion tool. Most sites do not allow any hard-pitched sales and marketing, which is in line with their objectives of building relationships and communication. Any strong marketing and selling tactics may result in your organization being labeled a spammer. Create value, not spam.

User statistics

Besides popularity, one of the main factors to consider is sites that appeal to your target audience. Sites like MySpace primarily target a younger audience of 18- to 29-year-olds and plenty from the music industry; therefore, you need to consider your target market before you choose one. Sites like LinkedIn primarily target an older audience of business professionals. Most social networking sites list user statistics on their site. You can also search online for information about these websites, along with their user demographics. As part of your marketing strategy, it is important to make sure you reach your intended target market.

Profile page

The social networking site must offer a well-designed profile page, which will be the focal point of your social networking strategy. This is the place to tell users what your organization is all about and where you'll include as much marketing "push" as you can.

CULTUREQUOTE»

"SOCIAL NETWORKING IS ALL ABOUT ACTIVE PARTICIPATION"

SOCIAL NETWORKING: DO'S AND DON'TS

Customers are increasingly influenced by social networks and blogs in their quest to find products and services, which makes social networking sites ideal marketing tools. In fact, the more that users participate on these sites, sharing their experiences about products and services they use, the more likely it is that you will be able to contribute to the success of your organization. The idea is to build and cultivate a good reputation on the Web.

Active participation

Social networking requires active participation. **DON'T** expect to connect with potential customers if you remain in the background. The secret is to invest enough time in interacting with customers and connecting with prospects. Like all good strategies, you get out of social networking what you invest.

Listen to feedback

Lending a keen ear to what customers have to say is essential in order to become successful at marketing through social networking sites. Customers will always voice their opinion, which is the best form of market research. **DO** identify people who lead conversations on these sites and lead them to participate in your campaign. In addition, **DO** contribute and post comments and feedback for other members as well. This is the best way to improve the visibility of your product or service in the process.

Conquer your fears

Many organizations fear that people may voice criticism about them through social networking. However, you have to understand that your brand image will always be at the mercy of those who share their experiences. Therefore, **DO** take an active role in promoting your brand image and addressing what people are saying.

Establish an online presence

Social networking sites can be used effectively to showcase your products and services and attract customers. More than just focusing on your organization's website, **DO** build up a social media presence to maintain a close connection with potential customers.

Find the right social networking site

It is vital to participate on social networking sites that are a match for your marketing campaign and goals. **DO** test a few, evaluate the results and stick to those that prove most effective for your organization's products or services.

Use tools

Social networking sites offer a variety of tools, so that you can save time on various tasks, which include sending updates to multiple social networking sites and responding to posts even when you are not online. However, **DON'T** make the mistake of using automated software to post generic comments or to send bulk messages. This is the quickest way to get kicked out of a community on a social networking site.

When building your network:

- **DO** keep your profile appealing, since that is what people see first when they search for you.

- **DO** keep adding fresh and valuable content to your blog page so that people have a reason to visit it regularly.

- **DO** dedicate times during the day to respond to messages and comments. This will let your customers and followers know that you take social networking seriously.

- **DO** be on the constant lookout for new contacts that are a potential fit and ask them to become part of your network. You can do this by sending friend requests, posting comments on their pages and returning comments left on your page.

SOCIAL NETWORKING: THE BENEFITS

There are good reasons why an increasing number of organizations and their marketing teams have turned to social networking sites as part of their marketing plan. The chances of success through online marketing are much brighter, due to social networking's far-reaching capabilities without the need for much financial investment. However, the time investment is great. Today, social networking sites are considered one of the most cost-effective marketing tools by organizations—catalysts through which you can open up a potential client base.

Blogging

Blogs are powerful tools that many organizations have discovered as the secret to their social media marketing success. Apart from marketing, blogs help you communicate with customers in the event of any issues. Moreover, blogs help to increase visitors to your website since they can be linked to each other and to your website. The more customers learn about you, and the more you provide valuable information, the more likely they are to trust you as a credible source.

Promoting sales

Social networking sites like Facebook and LinkedIn are the perfect platforms to promote sales. You will find many organizations promoting their products, sponsoring special deals and much more by creating groups, charity and business fan pages.

Marketing through video promotions

Websites like Facebook and MySpaceTV allow users to upload videos and share them around the globe. Audio and visuals have always been effective modes of communication and are best achieved through social media sites.

Keeping up-to-date on your industry

Organizations stay updated on current news and events that affect their industry through social networking sites. This gives them the opportunity to judge customer trends in their industry. In addition, organizations can reformulate their announcements and advertising strategies to retain customer confidence even if there is a negative wave affecting their industry.

Improving customer service

Customer service is one of the most important aspects of social networking. It is easy to answer customers' queries about your products or services. In addition, it portrays your organization as being readily available to help, giving a boost to the organization's brand image.

Gathering customer feedback and opinion

Social networking sites are great research tools. Customers leave their comments about products or services, and organizations can use these to monitor levels of customer satisfaction. Such comments also provide organizations with the opportunity to alter their product or service accordingly. Alternatively, customers can be asked their opinions on future products to help organizations gain insight, so as to create products and services that will be responsive to current and rising trends.

SOCIAL NETWORKING: SUCCESS STORIES

Organizations as large as Coca Cola, educational institutions and small business owners all have the same goal when it comes to social networking sites, which is to market their products and services to a large audience and interact with customers.

Coca Cola

The world's largest manufacturer of beverages isn't behind in unleashing the power of social networking sites as part of its promotional campaigns. One of its most successful campaigns was CokeTag, a bookmarking widget for Facebook. The social media application allows users to create customized Flash bookmark widgets that link to any topic that they are passionate about. This widget was to promote a project known as we8, a cultural exchange between top artists and designers from China and the West, in a run-up to the Beijing Olympics in 2008.

In 2010, Coca Cola used social networking sites like Facebook and Twitter in its Coca-Cola's Expedition 206 campaign. The company picked teams consisting of three individuals each to travel around the world in 2010 to visit the 206 markets that Coca Cola serves. Known as the "Happiness Ambassadors," the trio uploaded photos and videos of their travels to their Twitter and Facebook accounts. The winning team was selected by online voters on Facebook and Twitter. Along with the campaign, the company has reiterated the importance of maintaining accountability and transparency in its dealings with customers, making them a key part of the Expedition 206 adventure.

AT&T

Global telecommunications giant AT&T is active when it comes to social networking, with a strong presence on Facebook, Twitter, YouTube and Flickr. The company has a fan page on Facebook with more than 600,000 followers and links to special offers, latest AT&T news, information about its products and services, and a customer support page.

On Twitter, AT&T actively participates in microblogging with two accounts: ATTNews and ATTblueroom. The company also has a video channel, ShareAT&T, on YouTube, and posts regular uploads on topics ranging from college football to the latest in mobile technology.

AT&T also has a photo stream on Flickr, shareatt1's photostream, with four active groups and more than 5,000 photos uploaded. The company uses all these platforms to answer customer concerns through its support staff. In addition, AT&T actively promotes its participation in social networking on its websites and on its bills in an effort to encourage customers to use these services.

Virgin America

The airline Virgin America successfully uses social networking platforms such as Facebook, YouTube, Twitter and Flickr. The company gets travelers involved on its well-designed Facebook page. On the page, visitors can click links to search for flights and indulge in plenty of fun Facebook interactions. The page includes fan photos, fan videos, customer reviews, comments posted on the wall, a discussion board and company information. Users are also encouraged to interact with each other, making it easy to build relationships between the airline and its customers. Incidentally, the airline has also introduced a social networking service on its aircraft. The new system allows passengers to communicate on board with each other through their seat-back screens.

SOCIAL NETWORKING: INTEGRATION WITH OTHER MEDIA

To increase the effectiveness of social networking in their marketing strategies, organizations need to integrate their social networking pages as well as their websites. Earlier, most platforms allowed only customers to connect with each other, a strategy that worked for loyal customers but did little to reach new prospects. Social networking sites have now developed a variety of products that allow customers as well as prospects to connect by using the sharing features on each site.

Facebook, LinkedIn, MySpace and Twitter include sharing features and allow you to use embedded applications and widgets. The key is to integrate the most popular forms of social media into your website and allow people to spread the message. Twitter has applications such as TwitterFeed and TweetMeme that can be integrated on your website to encourage users to spread the message. Facebook has applications such as FBShare, Facebook Fan Widget and Facebook Connect Comments that can be added to your website.

There are tools that make it possible to post content to multiple social networking groups and monitor all from one place. These include TweetDeck on Twitter that allows you to post to Facebook, LinkedIn, Twitter and MySpace accounts. Versions are also available for the iPhone and iPad. Pluggio is another tool that integrates Facebook, LinkedIn and Twitter, as well as HelloTXT and others.

"PEOPLE DO BUSINESS WITH PEOPLE FIRST, ORGANIZATIONS SECOND"

SOCIAL NETWORKING SITES ARE EVOLVING

While you may take several steps to ensure that social networking works for you, it is important to remember that these sites are evolving in nature, with changes made on a daily basis. This is one of the things that attracts people to them. Therefore, your approach to using this medium must also keep evolving as these platforms do. Revisit your plan often and make improvements based on the actual results you are getting.

A secondary level for outreach is LinkedIn's Groups. Currently there are more than 150,000 groups, including business forums, alumni groups, fan clubs and conferences. If you run an interior design firm or sell to interior design firms, you can choose from nearly 90 groups catering to that field. Some are credential-based; some are based on geography. The group "owner" approves your membership to ensure validity.

Another way to build your credibility on LinkedIn is by participating in its Answers forum. For instance, if you are a travel agent, you might want to visit the Business Travel section to see whether you can give any advice. Use the soft sell. Approach the discussion as you would a face-to-face networking meeting. Of course people are there to further their businesses and make good business connections, but you need to get to know the person before promoting your services. Another tip: check out the person's public profile and Google him or her before engaging in a conversation. Chances are you might have a connection, whether it's a mutual friend, a college, a personal interest or a shared skill.

SOCIAL NETWORKING: KEY TAKEAWAYS

- Determine your marketing goals
- Spend time on research
- No hard selling
- Take a human approach
- Share photos and videos
- Test, measure and make adjustments

SOCIAL NETWORKING: HOW DO I GET STARTED?

The key to any organization's success in social networking is to define its audience, identify and locate potential customers, develop customer relationships and build a well-thought-of brand image. As a marketer, your organization's needs will determine how you utilize these sites to their full potential.

Download a step-by-step workbook for developing your social networking marketing plan.

Download the Connected Culture Social Networking Workbook FREE!

Visit: www.ConnectedCultureBook.com/freestuff
Enter in this code: networking-workbook

WHAT IS SOCIAL BLOGGING?

The term 'web log' was coined in 1997 by Jorn Barger. Soon after in 1999, Peter Merholz created the term 'blog' by shortening 'web log', the same way they shortened the name of Federal Express to FedEx. A blog is a special type of website, with entries or posts displayed in reverse chronological order. It's up to you what your blog contains; some use it like a diary, others for news or commentary on a niche subject that is of interest to their audience.

A blog is like an online diary that may contain images, graphics, videos and links to other blogs or websites. Readers can leave comments in response to what is written in the blog.

Blogs are one of the most effective ways to develop meaningful connections with your target audience and get real, honest feedback. They can also help improve search engine optimization (SEO). What's more, it's usually very inexpensive (or free) to get started. The difficult part is knowing how to make your blog effective and how to keep it in front of the right audience.

Brand image and credibility

When social blogging, remember that the content must be relevant, concise and must make customers aware about the new developments in your organization. What you are doing is building a brand image and your credibility. As a marketing professional, you know how important these two aspects are for your organization's product or service. You want to put your best foot forward and build a brand identity that screams professionalism and quality.

Pay attention to feedback

Using social media for marketing is a tough balance. The first thing you need to do is understand what is important to your customers. If your blog tends to change subjects often or tries to sell, you will only drive people away. The secret of using social media successfully is to concentrate on reaching the right customers with relevant communication. To engage your audience with one-on-one conversations. While your blog does the talking, you should be listening to your audience, as well. On blogs, readers have the option of posting comments. This is where you need to be listening. Many buyers will provide feedback of your product or service through these comments, thereby, making you more customer-conscious. Having a participatory approach will help you build a better image. Moreover, this will help you transform your organization to better meet customers' needs.

CULTUREQUOTE»

"ENGAGE YOUR AUDIENCE WITH ONE ON ONE CONVERSATIONS"

SOCIAL BLOGGING: TOP CHOICES

Choosing the right type of social blogging platform is essential in order to market your product or service efficiently. Not all platforms suit every type of organization, which is why marketing directors need to determine the right type. The best way is to gain insight into the most popular blogging platforms.

Typepad

TypePad is a social blogging platform available in several languages, with three levels of paid subscription. Marketing directors should take note of this one since several large organizations such as MSNBC, ABC, BBC and Sky News use TypePad to host their blogs. The good thing is that it is simple for beginners to use, without any technical aspects involved in creating a TypePad blog.

WordPress

WordPress is one of the most popular social blogging platforms. Setting up a blog on this site is easy, although it may seem a bit technical at first. WordPress has many user-friendly features and tutorials to teach you how to go about setting up a blog. Like some of its counterparts, WordPress is free to use. You can judge its popularity and effectiveness from the fact that over 300 of the biggest websites use it.

Blogger

Blogger, or BlogSpot, is another user-friendly platform from none other than Google. Like WordPress it is also free and is claimed to be the most popular social blogging platform. It also comes with your Google account.

Squidoo

Squidoo works well as a publishing platform and is a great way to connect with your customers. On this site you can create "lenses", or web pages, on topics and link them together to other pages. It is free and once you learn the process, it is fairly easy to use. The main advantage is that your organization can get the maximum exposure with a significant increase in traffic to your website.

HubPages

HubPages is more than just a blogging platform. Like Blogger, you can use it as a social networking site to help build up your network and link to other sites. HubPages is also free to use, making it a cost effective marketing tool to help you increase revenue.

Xanga

Xanga has evolved over the years, from a site for sharing book and music reviews, into a powerful social blogging platform. Members receive a website with a weblog, videoblog, photoblog and audioblog. In addition, members also receive a social networking profile, which is important for an organization. With tens of millions of users as of November 2010, there's no doubt there's something great about it.

LiveJournal

LiveJournal has a number of blogging features that work well when combined with its social networking features. The website has a user-friendly interface and simple tools to create effective blogs quickly.

Tumblr

Millions of people use Tumblr, a powerful social blogging platform that allows you to upload photos, text, images and video. One of the notable features of this site is that it allows users to 'reblog' their posts, which is a great way to gain further exposure.

OK, SO WHICH ONE DO I CHOOSE?

It is important that marketing directors don't just settle for the first social blogging platform. The key is to experiment and come up with a small list before making a decision. In addition, it may be beneficial to be part of multiple networks.

Not every social networking site is meant for every organization. The key is to determine which sites are best for you to post your blogs. One of the major factors to consider is the type of customers you are trying to reach. If you are a B2B organization, then you may be better off using Twitter, while if you sell consumer products, then Facebook is a viable option.

Alternatively, if you're looking for an SEO friendly fully functional blog then WordPress.org will give you complete control. However, if you want a more visual approach which includes pictures and graphics, then Tumblr or Xanga may be better options. Always keep the goals of your organization in mind.

Here are a few tips:

Ease of use: If you're an amateur blogger then pick an easy one like WordPress.com. Blogger and LiveJournal are also simple to maintain. TypePad is also relatively easy to use and you can set up photo

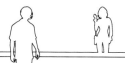

albums and add them to your blog. A lot of beginner bloggers also use Posterous which allows customization of styles, themes, domain mapping, multiple blogs and contributors.

The right result: Opt for platforms that offer community features. Blogger and TypePad have the potential to be ranked high by Google. Then there is MovableType.org, which is mainly used by businesses and comes at a nominal fee.

Customization: Some sites offer more customization than others. For example, you can control templates and remove advertisements on WordPress and LiveJournal. However, fully customizing TypePad will be difficult unless you are a seasoned programmer, although you can still use its wizards.

Cost: While some sites are dirt cheap or even free, such as WordPress, others will charge you for premium features. Then again, once you learn the ropes with social blogging you may want to host your own blog.

When you can identify what you need and want to accomplish from a social blogging network, it is then time to choose the right one for you.

SOCIAL BLOGGING: DO'S AND DON'TS

While an increasing number of marketing directors have realized the importance of social blogging, it is important to note that like all social situations, following certain etiquette is crucial. There are social marketing rules that you need to obey in order to build up your brand image and, most importantly, your credibility. The key is to plan your activities and use blogging tools correctly for maximum impact.

- **DO** use multiple social networks. Join networks that can help you drive traffic to your blog. Never rely on sticking to only one network.

- **DO** reciprocate. This is a good practice to improve your marketing campaign. Twitter users spread the word by re-tweeting your message. **DO** give back something in return. However, make sure it is quality content, or people will soon ignore you.

- **DO** ask for feedback from your readers. Merely being caught up in blogging won't help your marketing cause. Conduct a survey and obtain valuable feedback from your readers. Your survey must include space for readers to put in their comments and valuable suggestions. Once you do that, you can act upon it and change your marketing strategy accordingly.

- **DO** provide a unique story and content that is relevant to your product or service. The way you word your blog is important. For example, a blog about your organization turning three years old may not grab much attention. However, any discounts or an event you plan to throw for your customers will get you more exposure. Remember, the more valuable the content you provide, and the more optimized it is, the more likely search engines are going to give you a higher ranking.

- **DO** become a proactive blogger. Simply posting blogs will not help your social blogging cause. Take part in discussions and pay attention to what people have to say about your blog. The golden rule is to participate without pitching too high. Just be honest and share your ideas and concepts if you want to gain the credibility of your customers. DO build a lasting relationship with your customers.

- Blogging and having conversations online takes time. **DO** schedule time in your calendar for blogging on a regular basis. Do it during breakfast, lunch time, end of the day or at night. Do it whenever is convenient for you. But as with most things, if you don't put it in your calendar, it usually won't get done.

- **DON'T** stick to just one social network. Some organizations benefit from using social networks with less traffic but targeted to specific customers. Find the right social networks for your organization.

- **DON'T** take part in competitor bashing. This is one of the most important aspects to avoid in your blog. Your objective is to attract customers, so **DON'T** begin a cyber war with your competitors. Any silly move by your competitor can be commented on. However, don't resort to burying their posts and pretend to be a disgruntled customer. Never indulge in social media sabotage; it's something that could backfire on your organization and its reputation.

- **DO** focus on important issues. For example, if you are a manufacturer, writing about the best practices in your industry will help increase traffic and drive prospective customers to your website. Talking only about your organization, your product or service is a good way to lose followers.

SOCIAL BLOGGING: THE BENEFITS

It is great to see an increasing number of organizations, and marketing directors in particular, realize the importance of social blogging. In a recent study conducted by the Center for Market Research, an overwhelming 67% percent of direct marketers are more aware of the effectiveness of blogging as compared to just two years ago. Out of this, at least 45% have turned to active blogging, a trend which is likely to increase significantly over the short-term. The encouraging signs are that 44% intend to begin blogging in the near future. Even more exciting news is that 88% have tasted success with blogging and have witnessed an increase in demand for their products or services.

Microblogging

Social microblogging sites like Twitter have received the most response, with even Fortune 500 companies adding it to their blogging toolkits. Large companies such as Microsoft, eBay and Amazon seem to be among the most active bloggers on sites like Twitter, which is a hot favorite due to the concept of microblogging which requires the least amount of time. Moreover, Twitter has a large user base with more than an 80% success rate, which is why many companies prefer it as a marketing tool. Marketers are aware that once a customer is lost it costs significantly more to gain a new one. Customer service and retention is important, and microblogging sites allow organizations to be transparent. You will learn more about this in the following chapter on microblogging.

Listening in

Blogs are a powerful communication platform for individuals and organizations alike. One of the main reasons that organizations use social networks is to listen to feedback about their brand. This is a powerful and insightful opportunity. Companies such as eBay, Intuit and Amazon take the time to utilize feedback to improve on their products or services.

Market integration

One of the best aspects of using social blogging sites is that organizations are able to increase their opt-in list. Organizations can add a simple squeeze page (or web page) where prospective customers enter their email address to subscribe to their blog or email list. This has a greater overall effect on your marketing efforts and enables you to build a loyal following that you can communicate with.

Perceiving competition

Competition is what every marketer keeps a keen eye on. Through social media sites, companies assess how their competition is perceived and use that information to their advantage. Using social media as a research tool and to keep tabs on your competition is a great advantage.

Lead generation

Most organizations use social blogging as a way to generate leads. When you publish worthwhile content, it cuts through the noise. Customers love engaging content that carries value. This is your launch pad to create a conversation with prospects who are now interested in what you have to offer. As far as larger organizations are concerned, blogging remains more of a growth opportunity. You can communicate with your customers, receive feedback and get them to promote your brand.

Transparency

What organizations are also doing is building up a transparent image that helps foster trust in their customers. Marketing campaigns using social media are designed to build relationships—exactly what should be accomplished through blogging.

"IT'S NOT ABOUT SELLING. IT'S ABOUT CREATING VALUE FOR YOUR AUDIENCE."

— JERRY ALLOCCA

SOCIAL BLOGGING: SUCCESS STORIES

Social blogging is an effective marketing tool through which companies gain credibility, build employee relationships and build up a forum of communication with customers.

Seth's Blog

Seth Godin is one of the most popular names in social blogging. Having graduated from Tufts University and armed with an MBA from Stanford Business School, Seth went on to become a bestselling author of books such as *Free Prize Inside, Purple Cow, The Dip* and *Permission Marketing*. He founded an interactive direct marketing company called Yoyodyne and it was bought by Yahoo in 1998 for $30 million. In 2006, Seth Godin created Squidoo, a website which allows users to create 'lenses', or web pages, on different topics. Today, this grand master of social blogging continues to build online visibility and credibility through his blog at sethgodin.com or sethgodin.typepad.com. To all amateur bloggers he advocates the rule of the three 'U's—keep your blog Useful, Updated and Unique.

Cisco

One of the earliest starters in corporate social blogging was Cisco. When the mainstream media took note of Cisco's blog on China and its censorship, they decided to go ahead and implement social blogging as one of their marketing objectives with dedicated internal teams working on it. An August 30th, 2010 report states that Cisco saved $100,000 by launching a new product using social media. This included a mix of social blogging, online forums, video conferencing and 3D games. They were able to reach people in over 128 countries and save over 42,000 gallons of gas. With about 1,000 blog posts

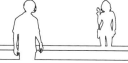

the impact of the campaign was tremendous and it cost ¹/₆th of a traditional product launch. With social blogging they have stopping talking 'at' their customers and have started talking 'with' their customers. Interactive communication has helped them build a stronger brand and engage their customers constantly.

Microsoft

Microsoft is not surprisingly one of the major companies to use a range of social network platforms including Facebook and YouTube to their advantage for the launch of their new phone, Kin. The campaign included 15 webisodes of a female personality travelling across America to meet friends she made on Facebook, Twitter and MySpace. These webisodes were professionally created to engage the audience. The next phase in the campaign was a series of live music events. Among the most important elements of their campaign was a page with a lively discussion on Facebook with videos and live events publicized on the wall. Twitter was used to promote the live events across all American cities along with tweets about the launch. Microsoft generated a large audience from its campaign on YouTube, with over 600,000 views. On MySpace the campaign continued with a page highlighting the webisodes.

The transparency and spirit is evident from the fact that Microsoft used its competitors' platforms like YouTube, rather than use its own platforms. The company responded to questions from its competitors and engaged in lively conversations on Twitter and Facebook. Their high quality videos and selection of characters added to the effectiveness of their marketing campaign. The important aspect was that there was no excessive mention of the product, which was mentioned in a relevant and natural way without being obtrusive. This is a perfect demonstration of the effective use of social media as a powerful marketing tool.

Dell

Dell is not shy about using social media to fulfill its marketing goals. The company has multiple Twitter handles, a Facebook page that is very active and a blog network, as well. In fact, Dell has made it known publicly that Twitter has given them a good return on investment. The company has managed to perfectly demonstrate that working on cross-platforms can lead to success. Their page on Flickr achieved one million views while their campaign for Direct2Dell included a YouTube channel with video content, which has given them over two billion contacts with customers worldwide. The @DellOutlet on Twitter has over 1.5 million followers while @DellOutlet brought in $3 million as revenue. The company's global reach through Twitter is more than $6.5 million in revenue. Among their strategies has been to streamline their presence on social media networks by creating meaningful content for their customers.

SOCIAL BLOGGING: INTEGRATION WITH OTHER MEDIA

While blogging is great, just adding a few posts every day to your blog will not get you noticed. For maximum impact, you need to publicize your blog using web 2.0 social networks such as Scribd, Xanga, Squidoo and Facebook, to name a few. Take a look at MySpace and you will find plenty of profiles of actors, artists, musicians and more. Many of them have set up their own blogs, too. This is one of the best ways to direct traffic to your website and get people to become aware of your product or service. Like any other social platform, customers use social media sites as a source of news and gossip. These sites attract millions of visitors and any blog posts you submit has the potential to reach those visitors in almost an instant.

Let's 'face' it. Facebook is undoubtedly growing into the world's largest social networking site with billions of page views per month and hundreds of millions of members and growing. The site allows you to bookmark links to your Facebook wall, which is a great way to drive traffic back to your blog. You can advertise your products on the site and link back to your blog as well.

Then there are sites, such as StumbleUpon and Digg where you can post your blog for thousands of people to see—and even vote on if your content is compelling and relevant. Good quality blogs will get you to the top pages of these social media sites and your popularity as a blogger can skyrocket.

Every site that you post to gives you a one way link back to your blog. Submit your blog to as many relevant sites as you can and automatically your one way links increase. Further, it's not just about spreading your blog around, it's about creating value and building credibility. When you integrate your blog with other social media sites, you become more visible online. Keep this up and aim to become an expert in your area of interest. Search engines love experts so you'll find that your rankings go up quickly.

Now just because this integration works well, don't go overboard. There are numerous social media sites out there. Pick a few to begin with that align with your goals and then focus your efforts on them. Maintain a disciplined approach so you can give your blog the right amount of exposure that will propel your organization forward.

What is Technorati?

The word Technorati comes from two words—technology and literati. It refers to technological intellectualism or intelligence. Created by Dave Sifry, Technorati is simply a search engine that helps you find blogs on the Internet. Lead411 recognized it as one of the hottest San Francisco companies of 2010.

Technorati indexes thousands of blogs in real time and offers them up as search results in a matter of seconds. Users can find opinions, top stories, videos, content and photos across technology, news, entertainment, politics, business, sports and more. This site tracks the influence and authority of blogs and indexes what and who is most popular in the blog world. The fact that it only publishes unique, original, edited and updated content adds to its credibility.

How do organizations use Technorati?

Every time you publish an article on your blog, Technorati indexes that information. Therefore, you need to claim your blog so you can modify and add to your Technorati blog listing. By adding some code to your blog, Technorati will recognize that this blog is indeed yours. Once this is done, you can configure your settings depending on what you want. For example, you can change the description and add keywords. Next you can create a meaningful profile that will tell the blog world who you are. This display showcases your blogs, tags and everything that's important to you. Technorati also allows you to add a photo. This is very important as blogs with photos get more prominence and will be read more often.

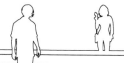

This site has a page called 'Technorati Blog Finder'. When you add the right tags to your blog, it will easily be found in the relevant blog category. For example, if your blog is about recipes then choosing the right keywords will ensure that your blog turns up in the listings for 'Blogs about Food.'

Readers who are interested in your blogs can create a watchlist so they can keep track of your future postings. By displaying all your claimed blogs you can help readers subscribe to different blogs that you host. Furthermore, if you have a website, you can put a link to your Technorati profile or Technorati Favorites widget so readers can read your latest posts. You can also place a search box so they can look for their favorite blogs. For any organization, Technorati enhances your online visibility by giving your blogs a stage.

SOCIAL BLOGGING: KEY TAKEAWAYS
- Determine the purpose of your blog
- Know your target audience
- Determine your category
- Frequently create quality content
- Register and be active on major social media sites
- Blogging for SEO

SOCIAL BLOGGING: HOW DO I GET STARTED?

It's essential to develop a social blogging marketing plan to use as a reference when you write new articles for your blog. Remember: blogging is at the center of social media and requires regular updates.

Download a step-by-step workbook for developing your social blogging marketing plan.

FREE STUFF!

Download the Connected Culture Social Blogging Workbook FREE!

Visit: www.ConnectedCultureBook.com/freestuff

Enter in this code: blogging-workbook

WHAT IS SOCIAL MICROBLOGGING?

A microblog is a shorter form of a traditional blog. Simply put, it's a web service that allows users to broadcast short 140 character messages to other subscribers of the service, like a status update. It announces what is happening in the microblogger's world at that moment, with the ability to link to more information on a blog, website, video and more.

The last couple of years have witnessed a significant increase in microblogging with several organizations using their messages for their marketing and PR activities. These short messages are sent and received via microblogging networks, which enables people who use the service to communicate and keep informed with what others are saying.

Analysts at Gartner Inc. have predicted that over the next few years, microblogging will be a standard feature on 80 percent of social software platforms on the market. The popularity of microblogging has attracted the attention of many organizations.

How are these messages relayed?

Microblogs are uploaded and transmitted through microblogging network services such as Twitter, Jaiku, Hictu and more. These short messages (140 characters including spaces) can be sent to other subscribers of the service, or to cell phones and other devices that are web compatible. For example, on Twitter, text-based posts are called "Tweets" and are displayed on the user's profile page. Users send and receive tweets via the Twitter website or compatible external applications such as smart phones.

One advantage of microblogging is that it makes interaction quicker. Instead of long blog posts and emails, short messages can be delivered more frequently to attract an audience of similar interests. Updates are, of course, instantaneous.

Is that all it takes?

If you are an organization looking to market your products or services, then using a microblogging platform can help you achieve your goal. To begin with you need to use a microblogging service like Twitter that will collect and publish the updates. People can choose to follow you and read your messages on the microblogging site or via their cell phones.

Why do it?

Microblogging can be a useful marketing tool by helping to create value for your audience while promoting your product or service. More than just broadcasting a message, you can stay connected with a large (and interested) audience, create a popular voice and personality for your brand and stay on your target market's radar. It's easy. All you need to do is sign up with a microblogging service and start typing. Keep in touch with your customers and potential customers and exchange information on whatever they're interested in. Many organizations and consultants have found microblogging a useful tool and have put considerable efforts into it. Poets, authors and entertainers have all found microblogging working to their advantage in a powerful, popularity-enhancing way.

SOCIAL MICROBLOGGING: TOP CHOICES

Marketing directors have a few choices when it comes to microblogging services. Twitter, with its famous blue bird logo, is currently the most popular service. Many may have heard of Twitter through the news or even know someone who is a frequent user. There are around 100

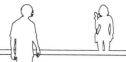

microblogging services worldwide that function in almost the same way as Twitter; the main differences are the terminology used, some of their features and the number of active users. For example, messages sent through Twitter are called 'tweets' while messages on Plurk are known as 'plurks'.

Twitter

Twitter has become the most widely used microblogging service. Its success can be attributed to many reasons including the fact that it allows third-party developers to make applications for it. Thousands of organizations both big and small are already exploring its effectiveness as a marketing tool. It's easy for a company to follow customers, listen to what they have to say and engage them in meaningful conversations through Twitter. This serves as a great platform to promote products and services to customers. It doesn't matter whether you are part of an organization manufacturing cosmetic products or an institute that conducts business management courses. Twitter will help you reach out to your customers, whoever they are and whoever YOU are. The main advantage of Twitter? It has more users than any other microblogging platform at the moment, boosting your advantage in reaching more people and more effectively communicating the latest news about your organization and industry.

Plurk

Plurk is another microblogging service for groups of people. The service has combined many features of other major microblogging sites as well as networking sites like Facebook. Notable features include the ability to enter different message types (not restricted to "what is happening now") as well as support for YouTube, Flickr and other social media sites. What's more, Plurk displays posts, or "plurks," in a unique horizontal timeline format.

Hictu

Hictu allows you to create microblogs with text, audio and video. This platform offers an easier way to create videos as part of a marketing promotion campaign. Once you sign up you can create videoposts with a webcam by simply clicking on the 'Record' button.

Sweetter

Sweetter is like Twitter—with a twist. This microblogging service allows users to vote for the posts, which is a good marketing tool and a great way to attract customers to the interesting posts you publish. While you can write what you please, remember: on this platform, it's other peoples' votes that will make your microblogs popular.

Jaiku

Jaiku is a microblogging platform that is currently popular in the Finnish community. However, since the service is now a part of Google, the chances of using it as a marketing tool in other communities are much brighter. The service has a user-friendly interface with the option of customizing designs.

OK, SO WHICH ONE DO I CHOOSE?

The best way to choose which platforms are right for you is to experiment with a few sites to determine which ones suit your organization's unique needs and goals. The old school of thought was that microblogging was simply a waste of time for anyone who is not a teenager. However, its growth among organizations wouldn't have been so rapid if there was no truth in its effectiveness as a marketing tool. Give it a try and spend a few weeks sending messages, listening and "following" others.

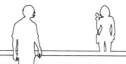

Factors that influence choice of platforms

Choosing the right microblogging service depends on whether a particular service is relevant to your organization. Another crucial factor is choosing the microblog platform your customers are already used to—and using. Microblogging was once aimed at the youth market and tech savvy community; however, there has been a significant increase in professionals and organizations becoming active microbloggers.

Weighing the pros and cons

From a marketing viewpoint, microblogs will help to build awareness about your organization and what it does. Regularly posting microblogs helps build up a brand image and is a great way to expand your network by building up contacts. In addition, they serve as a source of information and allow you to network with peers in your specific industry to help build better partnerships. Creating ads for marketing promotion campaigns is a long drawn out process, whereas microblogs give you the opportunity to regularly spread the word quickly and effectively. Besides, it is always good to know what your competition is saying, and what people are talking about regarding niche subjects.

Twitter is an ideal tool for non-profit organizations to draw attention to issues they cover in articles. For example, the World Wildlife Foundation uses Twitter to spread the word about endangered species. Department stores and fast food chains keep their customers informed through regular updates through microblogs on community events and topics related to their industry.

Sending out messages that reach customers through a handheld device or mobile phone makes it easier to reach a wider audience, even at a moment's notice. Sticking to interesting items that are specific to your industry will have customers reading, and paying attention to, your posts.

SOCIAL MICROBLOGGING: DO'S AND DON'TS

- When microblogging, **DO** be aware that part of a successful strategy is creating quality content in an effort to drive traffic to your organization's website.

- **DO** use a friendly tone for your product or service. This will help keep up the customers' level of interest and help you get more referrals.

- The aim of microblogging is to share relevant and valuable information, so **DO** make sure you keep up these goals in order to succeed.

- An important aspect of microblogging is to build credibility and relationships, which in turn will help your organization gain positive exposure. **DO** maintain this by helping others and having valuable conversations.

- When microblogging, **DO** follow best practices by posing questions, and answering some, too. Successful users on microblogging sites take time to engage in this practice.

- **DON'T** make the mistake of setting up your microblog so it sounds like a monotone dialogue. On microblogs people like to interact; one of the main goals of creating a microblog is to give your company a lively, interactive voice for communicating with customers.

- **DO** follow people. This is one of the keys to successful microblogging. Find people with similar interests as your organization and follow them. In addition, listening to others will do your marketing strategies a world of good.

- Microblogging isn't all about business-speak so make sure you don't build yourself a corporate brochure. **DO** be personable and interesting.

- Microblogging is a part of your brand building image so **DO** connect with people who talk about your brand in a positive or negative manner and reply to them accordingly. After all, this is a good way to perceive how customers are attracted to your product or service. More than just selling, microblogging is about listening and demonstrating good customer service.

- Very few people in this world like bragging. Instead of pushing your product or service, you need to share its features and benefits with your followers. **DO** keep them informed about special deals rather than just boast about the skills of your organization and its CEO.

- **DON'T** microblog too often and flood your followers with daily messages. The key is to engage directly with your followers over a reasonable timeline.

- As part of the whole exercise, **DO** monitor what your competitors are doing. Any issues or questions that users may have about your market should be addressed by you as soon as possible.

"FREQUENTLY CREATE, OR LINK TO, USEFUL AND INTERESTING CONTENT"

— JERRY ALLOCCA

SOCIAL MICROBLOGGING: THE BENEFITS

Platforms like Twitter have taken the concept of microblogging to a new level, helping organizations like Dell enjoy multi-million dollar increases in sales. However, as a marketer there is more to achieve than just increased sales.

Listening to customers

This is the best way to get feedback from your customers, which forms the base of your future business plans. Moreover, it opens an avenue for generating leads and opportunities.

Monitoring the industry and competitors

Microblogging lets you closely monitor your industry and competitors. This is the best way for them to remain updated and obtain valuable feedback as well.

Tracking conversations about competitors and their brands

Microblogging allows you to listen in on positive as well as negative comments about your competitors' brands. Keeping track of these conversations gives you a valuable edge and lets you compare your organization's strengths, weaknesses, opportunities and threats.

Grow sales

Through microblogging, organizations are beginning to build up loyalty for their brands with a focus on sales growth. Companies like Zappos and Dell have managed to significantly increase sales through Twitter.

Bolster brand image

Without overdoing the sales pitch, microblogging is the ideal way to boost an organization's brand image. Microblogging serves the dual purpose of gathering followers as well as spreading awareness about the brand.

Wooing customers with special deals and discounts

Microblogs are a highly effective way to drive traffic to your website. For example, you could send a microblog to your followers asking them to visit your website within 24 hours to take advantage of special deals and discounts. Amazon.com does this. The instant nature of microblogs makes them the perfect vehicle for time sensitive deals and messages.

Answering customers

Messages that are sent and received can be viewed on an organization's microblogging page, which is a good database of customer communications. This is your opportunity to have meaningful interactions with your customers. Respond to them, engage them, thank them and, perhaps most important, let them know you are listening.

Make customer complaints work for you

Organizations often ask, "what if a customer complains, and its out there for all the world to see?" Customer complaints are a gift. They allow microblogging organizations to "fix" the problem, make it "right," and build up trust in full view of the world. And if your customer has a problem isn't it better to know about it, then not? Negative comments also show transparency. When customers see the good and the bad, they know that you're real. Remember: your customers are talking about your brand whether you hear it or not. Isn't it better to encourage these conversations in an atmosphere where you're actively engaged?

Gathering followers

Organizations include a link back to their website from their microblogs. This is considered a backlink and aids in the overall picture of increasing search engine rankings. By growing your following you have the opportunity to expand your network and increase the amount of traffic and backlinks to your website.

Connecting with people in the industry

By following similar organizations, you can connect with other people in your industry and gather many valuable networking opportunities.

Engaging customers

Many organizations have found microblogging the perfect way to engage customers and update them with information. US Airways and Dell are among the top companies to set up shops on Twitter in order to market and sell their products and services.

Building up a knowledge repository

Building up a database is easy with microblogging tools. Organizations refer back to their own updates and messages, search for particular information and review their customer lists with the help of micro-blogging platforms.

Leveraging applications

A number of platforms like Twitter offer free applications that allow organizations to conduct a variety of useful business operations. For example, Twitter has twinfluence, an application that allows users to measure the influence of users and their followers. Organizations use this to monitor trends and influencers in their industries.

CULTUREQUOTE»

"BE INTERESTING"

SOCIAL MICROBLOGGING: SUCCESS STORIES

Successful organizations keep tabs on what their customers say about them on microblogging platforms. They monitor, discuss and evaluate microblogs as part of their marketing and PR activities.

Zappos

Among the companies to do remarkably well with social microblogging platforms is Zappos. The company has almost 200 of its employees on Twitter to keep up the company's brand image. Their campaign includes video blogging, as well. The short format on Twitter includes messages by employees about what they are doing at work. Included in their tweets are interesting information and resources about the Zappos website. The company's website has a page dedicated for Twitter, which is linked to every other webpage. The company's employee leaderboard indicates the amount of followers each employee has. What is prominent is the CEO's introduction which urges followers and their friends to join in. The company's transparency and openness is evident from the page that displays all the company's public messages from Twitter. In addition, Zappos has special pages to track tweets from customers. Marketing directors looking to increase their market exposure through microblogging should look at Zappos as a model.

Starbucks

Starbucks uses its Twitter account to share interesting events and music information with their customers. In addition, they address brand and charity related topics in order to reach out for client conversation. Over one million followers receive regular updates and news from Starbucks. The company has also participated in programs that allow advertisers to buy sponsored links on Twitter. The Twitter platform serves as the perfect engagement tool with customers who talk about Starbucks on Twitter, taking the company's customer relationship management efforts to a new level. Rather than just being entertained, followers of Starbucks on Twitter are engaged in the brand and discussions around it.

Starbucks has also brokered a deal with Foursquare. Foursquare is a mobile platform and social city guide where users can "check in" and share where they are at the moment. Starbucks offers special Barista Badges with discounts on drinks and food to Foursquare 'mayors' of retail stores.

Levi's Jeans

After successfully using Facebook as a tool for its sales and marketing initiatives, Levi's Jeans has engaged consumers through a follower, a 23-year-old USC graduate named Gareth, known as the 'Levi's Guy' on Twitter. Gareth has the responsibility of engaging in conversations about Levi's as a brand on Twitter. Gareth serves as the company's microblogging brand ambassador to help drive sales through his own actions and word of mouth. Gareth tweets about everything to do with the brand, from product launches to photo shoots and other news. To keep up followers' interest, fans are given gifts, invites and tickets to exclusive events.

In Australia and New Zealand, Levi's launched the Ispy Levi's campaign on Twitter where clues were released about the whereabouts of a few hand-selected people in signature jeans. After following clues on Twitter all day, customers had to ask the person if they were wearing a pair of Levi's. Those who spotted the person correctly were given Levi's jeans on the spot.

The Creme Brulee Man

While Starbucks and Levi's are from the big league, microblogging has brought success to smaller organizations, as well. In less than a year, Curtis Kimball has gathered over 12,000 followers on Twitter in a bid to popularize his food cart business. Call him a marketing genius or whatever you wish, Twitter is the only way customers can find his cart. Kimball's Crème Brulee Cart in San Francisco travels from one neighborhood to another, with regular updates on Twitter announcing the cart's location. In addition, customers are updated on the flavor of the day. All this allows Kimball to build up a personal relationship with his customers. Kimball also uses microblogging to engage his followers by asking them for suggestions on flavors and places he should appear with his cart.

SOCIAL MICROBLOGGING: INTEGRATION WITH OTHER MEDIA

One of the most effective ways of marketing is to use microblogging as the platform for entry to other social media sites such as Facebook and YouTube. Adding a link on microblogs to other blog pages on Squidoo, Blogger or Typepad helps drive even more traffic to your organization's website. Companies like Dell have two main pages on Facebook, namely, Facebook for Home and Facebook for Business. While Facebook for Home focuses on providing consumers with information about their products and services, Facebook for Business targets business customers. Both are linked through their microblogs on Twitter. Dell also has a presence on YouTube, LinkedIn and Scribd. With over $3 million in direct sales coming in through Twitter alone, Dell's integration with other social media sites earned them over $9 million in the past year.

Another way to integrate microblogging into other media is to add a Twitter widget (a small amount of code that performs a specific function) to your website. It can be a very effective way to get users participating in your Twitter updates. RSS, commonly known as Really Simple Syndication, is a family of web feed formats used to publish frequently updated works such as blog entries, news headlines, audio and video in a standardized format. An RSS document is called a feed, web feed, or channel and includes article headlines, summaries and links back to full-text articles on the web, plus metadata such as publishing dates and authorship. Web feeds benefit publishers by letting them syndicate content automatically. They benefit readers who want to subscribe to timely updates from favored websites or to aggregate feeds from many sites into one place.

SOCIAL MICROBLOGGING: KEY TAKEAWAYS

- Determine your goals
- Build up a community
- Create quality content
- Use application tools
- Make a commitment

SOCIAL MICROBLOGGING: HOW DO I GET STARTED?

There are several tools and strategies that help organizations create value and build up a large number of followers on microblogging sites. The following workbook will help you get started.

Download a step-by-step workbook for developing your social microblogging marketing plan.

Download the Connected Culture Social Microblogging Workbook FREE!

Visit: www.ConnectedCultureBook.com/freestuff

Enter in this code: microblogging-workbook

WHAT ARE SOCIAL VIDEOS?

Social video sharing sites allow users to upload and store video clips that can be viewed at any time. With faster internet connections and the advancements in mobile technology, video sharing sites have become increasingly more important. Videos can be produced, directed, edited and uploaded with ease. In addition, these websites allow users to create blogs and forums, making it as popular as photo sharing. Video sharing sites also double up as storage devices for videos that otherwise take up a lot of storage space. Videos can be captured and stored by following a few simple instructions.

Live streaming software enables videos to be viewed in real time, uploaded and shared on several social media sites. In the past few years, visitors to video sharing sites have more than doubled with the great demand for this service. Most sites offer great functionality to link and embed videos into other blogs and websites, making them ideal marketing tools.

Social video sharing sites have changed the way we view media. Today, even amateurs are able to steal the limelight. Whether you are searching for a clip from a movie, looking for some entertainment, a how-to video, or important news, it is easy to find on social video sharing sites.

Online marketers and advertisers have realized the importance of video sharing sites as a way to reach out to a wider audience. From artists to musicians and restaurants, video sharing offers a compelling and appealing way to create brand awareness. No matter what products or services your organization deals in, video sharing sites are an effective marketing tool.

SOCIAL VIDEOS: TOP CHOICES

Several social video sharing sites have their own unique features. However, it is important to understand the features of the popular sites prior to selecting one.

YouTube

YouTube is the most popular and widely watched video sharing service and is ranked the 2nd largest search network in the world. This is an indicator of how effective the site has been from a marketing viewpoint. Even politicians take advantage of YouTube's popularity, and presidential candidates have used the site to broadcast their speeches to a larger audience. Any organization looking to implement an online marketing strategy needs to pay attention to YouTube. The site is a clever mix of community and functionality. Users can watch videos on YouTube without having to become a member. However, the site has a very active community that interacts, comments and posts videos of specific interest. Members can comment and vote on their favorite videos, which is good for online marketing. The site has several customizable features that include screen size, playlists and much more. Some of the key features are the ability to embed videos on other sites, and create your own branded channel.

Dailymotion

Dailymotion is another popular video sharing site, and features videos that are more professional in nature, including newscasts, commercials and short films. The site allows videos to be uploaded from a webcam as well as mobile devices. The site's diversity of videos and its professional image attracts a large audience. However, marketers will need to ensure that their videos are of the highest quality since the competition is tough; many commercial videos are featured here.

Metacafe

Metacafe offers quality videos, and is carefully planned and laid out. The site has a dedicated review system to ensure that the highest standards of content are maintained. Videos are reviewed and approved by a panel of community members prior to being published online, which works well for the site's dedication to maintaining a clean, orderly and professional image. Metacafe does not post duplicate content, making it easy to find appropriate videos. Daily recommendations of popular videos are posted on the website's home page. In addition, there are plenty of categories and a thriving community that actively comments and rates videos.

Google Video

Google Video has one of the most searchable categories of any other video sharing site. Users can search for videos by category, rate videos, create playlists and comment on their favorite video clips. Google account users can use the same account to log into Google Video. The upload interface is easy to use, with settings to make videos public or exclusively for private viewing. A title and description can be added to the video to make it search engine friendly. The quality of content on the website is among the highest, which is why the website is very popular as a video sharing site. The site has a solid customer support base with a comprehensive FAQ section as well.

Break

Break is a video sharing site that has built up a good reputation by committing to specific types of videos. Apart from a variety of humorous video clips, there is plenty of content on entertainment, sports and the military. The website has built up a predominantly male user base, which marketers need to take note of. In addition to uploading videos, viewers can comment and rate video clips.

Other popular social video sharing sites include MySpaceTV, Yahoo! Video, Revver, Vimeo, vidiLife, Stickam, StupidVideos, blip.tv and more.

OK, SO WHICH ONE DO I CHOOSE?

Videos are meant to create compelling visual effects for your online marketing strategy. The best way to choose the right video sharing site is to note some of the top sites' best features and try a few before choosing one. Most offer free memberships, however this should not be a deciding factor in picking the right one.

Audience features

Video sharing sites must include features that make searching and viewing an enjoyable experience for the audience. Apart from a powerful search engine, the website must have the ability to search by category and offer previews of the videos. In addition, the site should allow users to submit video ratings and leave comments. The site must also permit a short description to be added to every video clip.

Producer features

Uploading videos should be easily accomplished on video sharing sites. The best sites offer plenty of resources to produce and post videos efficiently. In addition to video creation tools, the site must allow users the ability to select whether a video is public or private. The site should offer different ways of uploading content, including the ability to upload through cell phones.

Content

Video sharing sites should offer a large library of high quality content that is well regulated, without any copyright infringements, pornography, racist, or violent content permitted. This is one of the most important features to look for in a video sharing site. Sites that allow questionable material will not help your marketing efforts.

Ease of use

Video sharing sites should be easy to navigate, especially when it comes to uploading and posting descriptions. In addition, the categories should be well organized. One aspect that most users appreciate is no buffering delays, which can turn visitors away in an instant.

Customer support

It is important to choose a video sharing site that provides around-the-clock support through email, phone and a comprehensive user guide. Reading through the FAQ section of a website will give you a fair idea of how good or bad their customer support system may be.

Popularity

Although it is important to sign up with popular video sharing sites, it is essential to choose a site that has active members who interact, share and comment on a regular basis.

Storage limits

Each video sharing site has its own policies regarding storage limits. Therefore, it's smart to choose sites that offer better storage.

Video formats

Choose a site that supports the maximum number of video formats in order to ensure that your videos get the right exposure. These include WMV, ASF, QT, MOD, MOV, MPG, 3GP, 3GP2 or AVI and more.

"IF A PICTURE IS WORTH A THOUSAND WORDS, WHAT'S A VIDEO WORTH?"

SOCIAL VIDEOS: DO'S AND DON'TS

- **DO** make sure you have a marketing strategy in place and define your marketing goals prior to using video sharing sites.

- **DO** take the time to understand the policies of each video sharing site prior to logging in and uploading videos. By reading the rules of posting, you can eliminate the risk of being banned from the website.

- Spamming is not tolerated on any social video sharing site. Make sure you **DON'T** post any duplicate content, which is also considered spam. Most sites have an efficient administrative team that will flag you as a spammer and blacklist you from the site.

- **DON'T** make the mistake of pushing your products or services directly with hard selling. Uninformative commercials that have no entertainment value are frowned upon by most video sharing sites.

- **DON'T** use any specific software program that artificially brings visibility to your video. This will result in instant removal of your video from the website.

- Social media demands that you provide regular content. **DO** provide quality video content on a regular basis.

- The key to success is to remain active on video sharing sites. **DO** comment regularly on other peoples' videos. However, remember to refrain from spamming or blatant selling.

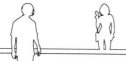

- With every video, **DO** add links and promotions to your video in order to implement a successful marketing strategy.

- **DO** make sure the video title is interesting and contains popular keywords if possible.

- **DO** direct viewers from your blog to video sharing site links and vice versa.

- **DON'T** post videos in the wrong category, which defeats the purpose of driving traffic to your website.

- **DO** allow members to post on your wall and leave comments.

- **DO** thank members for responding to your videos and comments.

- **DO** send and accept friend requests you receive on video sharing sites.

- **DO** choose your communities carefully so that you end up targeting the right audience.

- **DO** keep your profile live and updated.

SOCIAL VIDEOS: THE BENEFITS

Unlike television, video sharing sites offer a cost effective way for organizations to upload their commercials at a fraction of the cost. Besides being kind on your budget, there are several other valuable ways your organization can benefit.

Increasing online presence

Social video sharing sites are an effective way to reach out to a large audience. Videos attract visitors, which in turn has the potential to generate a great deal of traffic to an organization's website. Video sharing sites are search engine friendly and have the potential of driving traffic to a website.

Building brand image

Adding video to your marketing provides the perfect boost to your organization's efforts in building a brand image. This can be achieved without overdoing the sales pitch or the use of hard marketing tactics. Sharing videos creates a greater impact on customers than many other marketing tools can.

Listening to customer response and feedback

Users are allowed to post comments and feedback, providing organizations with a comprehensive database of how customers perceive their products or services. This is a useful tool to formulate future business plans and respond to customer queries and feedback.

Targeting new customers

Video sharing can have a tremendous impact on potential customers. Visuals provide the perfect opportunity for customers to want to visit an organization's website in order to learn more about its products or services, and ultimately make a purchase.

Providing accurate information about products

Video sharing sites assist organizations in presenting an accurate idea about their products or services in a way that is far more impactful than just text and photos alone. Once potential customers are aware of the details in a high impact way, they are more likely to go ahead and make a purchase.

Promoting special deals

Video sharing sites enable organizations to reach out to a large audience and keep them informed of any special deals on their products or services at a fraction of the cost of advertising on TV. Giving customers firsthand knowledge of special deals and discounts on the product through video presentations is more likely to have an impact on sales.

Targeting specific customers

There are a large number of categories on most video sharing sites. These categories are well organized and help organizations better target specific customers.

"A VIDEO CAN BE A LISTING IN A SEARCH ENGINE"

— JERRY ALLOCCA

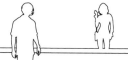

SOCIAL VIDEOS: SUCCESS STORIES

The Muppets Studio

One of the companies to use video sharing sites successfully as a marketing tool is The Muppets Studio. The company leveraged the power of video sharing through YouTube to bring back The Muppets Show, which declined in popularity quite some time ago. The studio created a YouTube channel with exclusive picks featuring the best humor from the show. Since its launch, their channel gained over 400,000 views, over 110,000 subscribers and more than 3,500 comments on its page. The studio used YouTube's comments and annotations in these video clippings. In addition, there are clips of The Muppets on cooking shows and other mobile applications. The studio's YouTube campaign managed to successfully rejuvenate the brand in a big way.

University of Phoenix Online

With broadband speeds increasing significantly, online education programs have become popular. The University of Phoenix Online is another organization that harnessed the power of social video sharing with video testimonials, webisodes, mini-documentaries and reviews featured on YouTube. Although building a subscriber base is not important for the university's marketing strategy, the video clips have over 700,000 views. The university has one video to connect with each potential student that visits their channel or searches for an online school. The idea behind launching several videos is to increase the chances of a prospective student finding a student that they can identify with. Testimonials by MSNBC Anchor and graduate, Christina Brown, are among the most watched videos on YouTube. In addition, the university has a large number of viewers for a mini-documentary series that features inspirational stories about real life experiences by graduates from the University of Phoenix Online. Along with the videos, the university has used compelling content in order to convert prospects into enrolled students.

The Home Depot

Home improvement videos have always been a major hit with audiences, and The Home Depot has taken the opportunity to use video sharing sites like YouTube and the popularity of how-to videos to publish content relevant to their brand. This has been achieved without any hard selling tactics, but in the form of educational content. Through these videos the company has been able to establish itself as a trusted source for home repairs and renovation. They also manage to promote products and tools without the usual commercial pitch. The company also features its employees in the tutorials, presenting the right human approach which has a positive effect on marketing. The videos offer practical knowledge and tips on how to save money on home improvement ventures such as replacing a toilet and re-tiling a bathroom. Notable from a marketing viewpoint is the company's simple design and layout with a custom background image, unlike other users in their category.

SOCIAL VIDEOS: INTEGRATION WITH OTHER MEDIA

Social media provides the opportunity for different channels to blend in order to become one comprehensive interactive marketing strategy. Most organizations look at social video sharing as part of their cross-promotional efforts to launch an online marketing campaign.

Customers are the main target when it comes to marketing on social video sites, making it essential for organizations to invite customers to participate in YouTube viral marketing video contests. These contests can highlight real consumers providing their testimonials about the products or services. In addition, a link can be included to a YouTube video tutorial when sending out purchase-confirmation emails. To integrate YouTube videos, you can use the 'Embed' code provided by YouTube. All you need to do is copy and paste the code in order to place the video on your webpage or blog.

Considering how people share information on the web, it is essential for organizations to integrate social media with their website. Integrating various social media platforms with each other lays the foundation for a successful campaign. Video sharing sites need to be considered as an ingredient in a comprehensive marketing strategy.

SOCIAL VIDEOS: KEY TAKEAWAYS
- Determine your goals
- Create quality video content
- Create an optimized title and description for your video
- Search for friends
- Help others

SOCIAL VIDEOS: HOW DO I GET STARTED?

Participating in video sharing sites does not require much expertise. The following workbook contains several easy steps to help you get started.

Download a step-by-step workbook for developing your social video marketing plan.

Download the Connected Culture Social Videos Workbook FREE!

Visit: www.ConnectedCultureBook.com/freestuff

Enter in this code: videos-workbook

WHAT ARE SOCIAL PHOTOS?

Social photos—commonly known as photo sharing—are digital photos that are published (or posted) online, enabling users to share them, and comment on them, with others publicly or privately.

Remember the previous chapter about blogs (those online avenues of self-expression and ideal vehicles for launching marketing campaigns)? As you may recall, blogs invite readers to participate and comment in a forum that also helps drive visitors to websites. Add digital images to these blogs and you get photoblogs, which can be uploaded on social photo sharing websites such as Photobucket, Flickr, Picasa, Fotki and others.

With the advancements in mobile phone technology, users can take photos on mobile devices and transfer them instantly to photoblogs. Social photo sharing sites include tools to edit, organize, add text, store and link photos and text to other websites. This helps get your posted images viewed and also retrieves results from search engines, which increases your organization's online exposure. The New York Times launched its photoblog in 2009, to enormous success and increased traffic to its website. Many organizations use social photo sharing sites as part of their Search Engine Marketing strategy because it allows others to find out about their organization through searching on sites like Google Images.

The advantages

One advantage of social photo sharing sites is that descriptions, titles and keywords can be added to the photo albums and linked to a website or a blog. In addition, these photos can be used as a slideshow, making it an ideal marketing tool. It also allows photos to appear in search engine results, which helps your visibility. Photo sharing sites enable users to add a direct link to their website from the image itself.

Photo sharing sites offer users a convenient way to manage and organize their photos. Over time, photo sharing has expanded significantly thanks in part to websites like Flickr, which offer a variety of features including organizational tools, editing functions and a large amount of online storage space. Today, photo sharing has spread beyond the internet to mobile devices and social networks like Facebook. Because cell phones are equipped with MMS (Multimedia Messaging Services), sharing photos is easier than ever. With photo sharing sites, marketers have a valuable tool for marketing campaign launches.

CULTUREQUOTE»

"A PICTURE IS WORTH A THOUSAND WORDS."

SOCIAL PHOTOS: TOP CHOICES

Photo sharing has become an integral part of social networking sites—sites that have changed the way people connect. Social photo platforms allow users to share photos and links with anyone they wish.

With hundreds of photo sharing sites available today, choosing one can seem like a daunting task. To save you time, here's a list of the top photo sharing sites. Explore them and discover which ones best suit your organization's marketing needs.

Flickr

Flickr is one of the most popular social photo sharing sites, and currently hosts over 5 billion images. Users are allowed to integrate pictures in a photo stream along with notes about the images. Apart from photos, Flickr also allows video hosting. Bloggers can upload images they embed in blogs and other social media. While uploading photos, the website allows you to add a title, a description and a tag, and to set security levels for the images. Tags help other users to search and locate images easily. Photos can be shared privately or with the entire Flickr community. Users can log in from their Yahoo account (Flickr is owned by Yahoo) or create a new Flickr account. In addition, users can connect to other social media sites and send updates to those sites, as well. In addition, the website has several features including "drag and drop."

Fotki

Fotki is a digital photo sharing site with an easy to use interface. Apart from creating photo galleries, videos can be uploaded. The site has a built-in geo-mapping feature to connect images with Google Earth. Those looking for a variety in photography frequent the site, which has a number of features that include tagging, social bookmarking and more. Paid account holders can enjoy unlimited storage space for digital images. Included are a host of community tools for tagging photos and videos, profiling, and photo and member search options. With over 1.6 million users, Fotki is a good site for sharing photos, as well as selling prints and online printing.

Photobucket

Photobucket is another site for uploading, sharing and linking photos and videos. Users can store thousands of photos free and share them on other social media sites such as Twitter and Facebook, among others. Uploaded photos can be edited for special effects with the site's photo editor. Photo albums created can be accessed on mobile devices or on smart phone applications provided by Photobucket. Users can search for images and videos from among the site's large database. One of the notable features is the built-in organizer to keep photos and videos well organized.

Picturetrail

Another photo sharing site with a variety of features is Picturetrail. The site offers free basic accounts with a limitation on storage of photos and videos, while premium or paid accounts have unlimited storage. Other features include photo sharing slideshows, conversion of photos to digital postcards, and statistics that indicate how many users have looked at your pictures.

Photoblog

Photoblog is easy to set up and has a variety of themes. The site offers photo sharing which is set up in a blog style. Blogging is an exclusive feature of Photoblog and includes a wide selection of photo stories by millions of users.

Picasa

Picasa is a photo sharing and editing application from Google. Like all Google's products, the site is packed with features and plenty of online storage space. Other features include geotagging, which is associating a photo with a location. Picasa can also be downloaded to a user's desktop for convenience while photos can be stored online. Apart from Windows, the application can be used on a Mac and Linux systems, as well.

Facebook

Among the most popular social photo sharing sites is Facebook, with over 500+ million users across the globe and more photos than any other site on the internet as of November 2010. Images can be uploaded on the website with reasonable file size limitations. Like several other social media sites, Facebook allows users to link their account to other social media sites. Facebook offers personal and business accounts and plenty of opportunities to advertise on the website.

And more...

Other social photo sharing sites include Tabblo, dotphoto, fotolog, and Faces, among others. Each site has its own unique features that need to be tested prior to choosing one that suits your organization's needs.

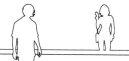

OK, SO WHICH ONE DO I CHOOSE?

Size matters

Besides gaining exposure on the web, organizations have the opportunity to solve their storage problems since these websites offer plenty of online storage space. Moreover, it is easy to manage and organize photos on sites like Flickr, Photobucket, and Fotki. Free services offer less storage space as compared to paid sites. Organizations will most likely prefer a paid service that offers more storage space and a wide variety of features. Most paid services are typically not very expensive.

Features

One of the important factors to consider when looking for a photo sharing site is its features and how well they will serve your marketing strategies. Many websites offer online galleries, printing services, slideshows, and more. The more features you require the more you will have to pay. However, the exposure you receive on the web is well worth the cost. It is essential to choose a service that offers a high quality gallery option so that the photos can be well presented to potential customers.

Credibility of the website

There may be hundreds of photo sharing sites; however, it is important to consider opting for a popular and credible company. There are some who enter the market and fade away in a few months or years. Websites like Flickr and Facebook have millions of users and are among the most popular photo sharing sites today. It would be prudent to keep backups of all the photos you post just in case the company you choose fades away—along with your digital images.

Security and password protection

If you don't want to share with the public, one of the features to look for is the ability to password protect your photo galleries. Using this feature helps to prevent any misuse of your photos by the public.

Standalone applications vs. browsers

While some websites allow photos to be uploaded online, standalone applications are faster and easier to use. Websites like Picasa include a desktop application that does not require the use of a web browser to upload, organize and manage photos. These standalone applications are the easiest way to upload multiple photos online.

Display options

Most photo sharing services offer a variety of display options including photo size. It is important to choose one that allows large or small photos to be uploaded, depending on your requirement. In addition, make sure the site has slideshow options, which is the best way to display a gallery of photos.

Quality expectations

When it comes to marketing, there can be no compromise on quality. Each site will have a difference in its photo book quality. You need to make sure that the quality of the photos is not compromised when uploaded. Only the highest quality photos should be viewed by other users.

Protecting your photos

Photo sharing has become increasingly popular over the years and is a great way for organizations to communicate with their customers, but with the popularity of photo sharing there has been an increase in photo

theft as well. Fraud and photo theft can be prevented with the use of watermarks, which is text superimposed on the image you are uploading. These watermarks indicate ownership and the rights of the photos.

Integration with social media sites

The best photo sharing services facilitate interaction with other users and allow them to comment, but they also enable easy integration with other social media sites.

Help and Support

Support in the form of FAQs, tutorials, web forms and telephone assistance are the essential elements of a good photo sharing site. Make sure the service provides adequate help and support around-the-clock.

So...how do I start?

The best way to choose a photo sharing site and to start enjoying the benefits is to sign up for a free account with two or three sites and upload a group of pictures. This will give you an idea of how easy it is to upload to each site. Start a gallery with each site to see how their interface works. The one you find comfortable navigating, and that meets your organizations goals, should be the one to pick.

SOCIAL PHOTOS: THE BENEFITS

Social photo sharing sites such as Flickr can be a valuable platform for organizations to connect with existing and potential customers as long as they go about it in the right manner. Many organizations have realized the benefits of photo sharing sites as part of their marketing strategies. Here are some of those benefits:

Participating in communities

For organizations, the purpose behind using photo sharing sites is to gain exposure for their products or services. Many photo sharing platforms offer the opportunity to join groups or communities that suit an organization's niche. These groups are where many organizations actively participate.

Building an online presence

Through photo sharing, organizations are able to create links to their website and increase traffic. These sites allow blogs and links to be added to photo galleries, increasing the chances of building up a greater online presence. Photos can also be tagged, which means they have better visibility and are likely to generate more user comments.

Brand image

Joining photo sharing sites is the perfect exercise in building up a brand image. Organizations tend to build their brand image when they actively participate on websites like Flickr. Moreover, it is human nature to be attracted to visuals and associate them with a particular brand.

Taking advantage of multimedia services

Some photo sharing sites allow videos to be uploaded, making it the perfect platform for presentations to be distributed to millions of customers at a fraction of the cost. An increase in bandwidth and storage capacity works in favor of those seeking to take advantage of multimedia as a marketing tool. In addition, organizations avoid the expense of having to post multiple photos via email and run costly campaigns on other forms of media.

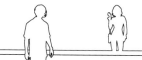

Managing multiple projects

Photo sharing is a cost effective way to manage multiple photo projects from one location without having to set up a private network. Multiple co-workers and associates can view and make changes to a photo project without having to physically be in one location.

Listening to customer feedback

Photo sharing sites allow users to comment and leave their feedback, which works in favor of organizations who want to fine tune their products or services according to the needs of customers.

Customer base as an image stream

Organizations can use photo sharing sites to show off their customer base as an image stream.

SOCIAL PHOTOS: DO'S AND DON'TS

- While social photo sharing has become a powerful and effective marketing tool to engage with customers, **DO** follow the rules of social media and social etiquette when using these sites.

- Photo sharing sites are vast social networks, therefore **DO** remain respectful and polite and offer lots of positive comments and constructive criticism. This is also a good way to build up a loyal following.

- **DO** maintain a contact group with other photographers and bloggers who have a good reputation and made a good impression on you. A personal rapport with other users is a good way to increase your network and get potential customers to your website.

People that add you to their contact list are likely to keep track of you so don't hesitate to add them to your list.

- **DON'T** forget to reply to comments from other users. You can also search through their photos and add comments, as well.

- When someone adds your photos as a 'favorite' to their list, **DO** reciprocate and add some of their photos to your 'favorites' list if the photos are a good "fit." If someone leaves positive comments, **DO** add that user as a contact.

- Like other social media sites, social photo sharing sites enable users to leave comments. This is the best way to build up a relationship with potential customers. **DO** take comments seriously and reply to them whether they are negative or positive.

- Whenever you receive group invites, **DO** take the time to find out more about the group's activities and then consider joining them. If the group is relevant to your niche, **DO** join up and submit images immediately. It doesn't hurt to participate in a group that could lead to potential customers coming your way. Groups have their own set of rules on postings, so make sure you abide by them.

- A great way to build up a following is through testimonials. If you do receive one in appreciation, **DO** return the favor whenever possible.

- Pay great attention to copyrights and **DON'T** use somebody else's photos. Most photo sharing sites have an "All Rights Reserved" option, which indicates that you don't have the authority to use them

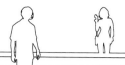

without permission. Sites like Flickr have a "Creative Commons" license, which means you can use a photo by following certain rules.

- For security purposes, **DO** password protect photo galleries that you do not wish the public to view.

- **DO** add links back to your website when uploading photos to the site. This will help increase traffic to your website.

- **DO** become an active member once you sign up with a photo sharing site. It adds credibility to your organization and helps build a following rapidly.

- **DO** keep your photos and blogs interesting. You want readers and followers to become your potential customers. Therefore, cover what your audience's needs and wants are. That is what customer service and marketing are all about.

- **DO** get involved and stay involved in social photo sharing. The aim is to get your organization's name out there and build up your brand image.

"IT'S HUMAN NATURE TO BE ATTRACTED TO VISUALS AND TO ASSOCIATE THEM WITH A PARTICULAR BRAND."

— JERRY ALLOCCA

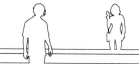

SOCIAL PHOTOS: SUCCESS STORIES

Social photo sharing sites may not be as popular as other social media sites like Facebook and Twitter. However, there are many organizations that are using photo sharing sites to their advantage.

BBC

Among the most successful brands to embrace social photo sharing sites is the BBC. The company has spaces on Flickr for fans to upload photos. These photos are linked back to BBC websites and integrated with multimedia properties. Among the photo galleries posted by BBC include:

- *The One Show* with over 800 members and 2,582 photos
- *Eurovision* with 78 members and over 900 photos
- *Football World Cup* with 154 members and over 800 photos
- *At the Fringe* with 31 members and over 550 photos
- *Rugby World Cup* with 94 members and over 500 photos
- *Electric Proms* with over 20 members and 125 photos

Nikon Digital Learning Center

Nikon Corp. is a world leader in digital imaging and takes full advantage of social photo sharing sites as part of their marketing campaign. The Nikon Digital Learning Center on Flickr by the Nikon School was launched in August, 2007. The group now has over 54,000 members and over 440,000 photos on Flickr. The group offers Flickr members practical tips on photography from Nikon professionals and conducts a series of tutorials. Apart from their own brand of professionals, there are a number of sponsored professionals in the group who answer questions posed by other Flickr members and also share their personal experiences. The group has three resident professional photographers and a few technical managers that contribute to the group. Members of the group are allowed to contribute photos, participate in discussion threads and tag photos.

Urban Outfitters

Urban Outfitters, a clothing giant with multiple store locations across the globe, launched the Urban Outfitter's Flickr group which was initially promoted from their blogs and website. The group has over 3,400 members and over 7,700 photos uploaded on the group's page. The collection of photos includes some from their own clothing line, and members are allowed to upload their own Urban Outfitters photo shoots. The company's European branch has its own group on Flickr, Urban Outfitters Europe.

SOCIAL PHOTOS: INTEGRATION WITH OTHER MEDIA

There are plenty of ways for organizations to market their products and services using social photo sharing sites. The main objective is to build up awareness among other members of these websites about your organization's products and services.

Integration with Facebook

Most organizations go about using websites like Flickr by uploading photos and then integrating them on another social networking site like Facebook. The main advantage is that pictures posted on Flickr can be found by anyone searching on the web, whereas photos published on Facebook can only be found by subscribers of Facebook.

Integration with Twitter

Organizations can successfully promote their websites by using Flickr and Digg. The sites enable users to build up an interactive base, share images, and join in discussions. Photos must be relevant to the type of business in order to attract the right customers. In addition, when photos are uploaded to Flickr, messages can be sent out on Twitter. Flickr allows integration with Twitter through the Flickr2Twitter application. Posts can be uploaded to Flickr and Twitter simultaneously or through tweets if photos are already on Flickr. Photos that are geotagged can also be included in Twitter messages.

SOCIAL PHOTOS: KEY TAKEAWAYS

- Determine your marketing goals
- Create a profile
- Join communities or groups
- Upload high quality photos
- Commenting on other people's photos
- Creating links

SOCIAL PHOTOS: HOW DO I GET STARTED?

Organizations can use photo sharing sites to reveal how their products benefit customers, to highlight corporate events, to make announcements to employees and customers and more. Get started with this planning tool:

Download a step-by-step workbook for developing your social photo marketing plan.

FREE STUFF!

Download the Connected Culture Social Photos Workbook FREE!

Visit: www.ConnectedCultureBook.com/freestuff
Enter in this code: photos-workbook

WHAT IS SOCIAL NEWS?

Social news sites allow users to submit and vote on news stories. Social news sites offer the opportunity for your organization to share content relevant to your industry, and they allow you to participate in discussions with other social news site members.

For marketing directors, social news sites are powerful tools for driving viral marketing. They attract the attention of customers, drive traffic and build links to an organization's website. Most importantly, they help expose an organization's website content to a larger, more diverse audience. News stories, articles and videos can be submitted to these sites and shared with other users. Readers are allowed to vote on the content submitted, which is a great way for an organization's website to gain more visibility. Apart from votes, some social news sites have editors to determine content for its newsworthiness. In this way, irrelevent stories may be removed from the website.

How do social news sites work?

Social news sites use algorithms or formulas to determine the popularity of each story, or page, submitted by users. The popularity of a story varies according to a number of factors. Larger social news sites use a variety of algorithms, while smaller sites do not. The purpose behind using algorithms is to prevent manipulation of content by unfair practices.

SOCIAL NEWS: TOP CHOICES

Social news sites can be categorized into two types of communities: those that focus on a diversity of topics, and others that cater to a specialized, niche audience. Marketing directors need to pick the right social news communities to promote their website because the community that you choose depends on your organization's marketing objectives.

Digg

Digg is among the most popular social news sites. The site shifted its initial focus from technology to a variety of topics such as politics, education, entertainment, humor and much more. Users that find a page they want to share can submit the URL to the site. Other users have the option of either voting for the article (known as a 'digg'), or voting against it (which is known as a 'bury'). Submissions with the highest votes are displayed on Digg's home page, with an increasing number of people likely to click on them. For organizations, this is an ideal tool to drive traffic to their blog or website.

Reddit

Reddit is a popular social news site that focuses on a wide range of topics including politics, business, science, programming and even regional based topics. Users, known as 'redditors', can submit articles or links to content on the internet, which other users can vote on. Articles with the most number of votes are posted on the front page. Users are also allowed to comment on links and reply to other comments. One of the notable features of Reddit is that users can create their own categories, known as subreddits. For marketers, it is important to note that the front page of Reddit can generate thousands of hits for their website.

Fark

Fark is a social news site that allows users to post unique stories from around the world. Users are allowed to comment on articles that are posted on the website once approved by the administrators. What makes the site stand out is that its content is frequently used as a humorous source for news by radio stations and late night comedy shows.

Links are submitted by Fark members, referred to as "Farkers." Moderators can approve or "greenlight" the links for posting on either the main page or one of the inner pages. Greenlit links can generate thousands to hundreds of thousands of page views for the recipient, which can generate an enormous amount of traffic to your website in a short time.

Mixx

This social news site lives up to its name and has a category for all types of news including business, travel, politics, entertainment, home improvement, and much more. Users have the option of creating groups to share news with other users. Mixx allows users to search for relevant content and interact with other users who share common interests. Content can include text, images and video. The website is in partnership with major online publishing outlets such as Reuters, CNN.com and USA Today. Users have the right to vote and comment on all articles that are published.

And then there's niche...

A number of niche sites such as Techmeme, which features tech news, Sphinn, for internet marketing news, and socialnews.biz, featuring business news, are among the new players in social news. Here are some of the larger, more popular niche social news sites:

Slashdot

Slashdot is a social news site exclusively related to science and technology. Stories have a "comments" section that is moderated by a user-based moderation system. To date, Slashdot has over 5.5 million visitors per month and is the winner of 20 awards.

Showhype

Showhype allows users to share and discuss news related to entertainment. Bloggers can submit and maintain blogs that can be uploaded to the website for free. The site also allows sharing of links and videos from other websites. Users can vote for articles, blogs and links, which is a great way to drive traffic to an organization's website. I Am Bored, Shoutwire, Newsvine, Sphinxx and NewsCloud are a few of the other popular social news platforms that focus on specific types of news, meeting marketing goals by creating incoming links and driving traffic to websites.

OK, SO WHICH ONE DO I CHOOSE?

To start with, explore the social news sites that contain information relevant to your organization and your target market. Also, **listen to feedback.** Bloggers often write about the success they have achieved through specific social news sites. It's a good idea to do a background check on social sites through a quick blog search on Google. Your research can also include asking more experienced users for their opinions.

Once you begin exploring, make sure the site you ultimately choose to blog on has:

An active community

To benefit your organization, a social news community must have a sufficient amount of active users, resulting in better traffic to your website. Most of the popular sites such as Digg and Reddit offer many news categories and volumes of daily users.

Regular updates

It is important to choose a social news site that is regularly updated. There is no point in joining a community that does not keep its content constantly fresh and current.

Abundant commenting and voting

It is easy to find the right niche once you do a bit of research on the top social news sites. The first thing is to note how many comments each news story has on a site. Next, check out the number of votes required to reach the website's front page. Those that have a reasonable number of votes will be worth trying.

Frequent submissions

Choosing sites that frequently publish new stories is essential. This also increases the competition to make it to the front page. Stories on the front page should also be fresh and have relevant content.

Large member communities

A large community will always increase the chance of improving traffic to your website. Besides, it makes good marketing sense to get seen and heard among a number of active members on a social news site.

A relevant niche

Many sites cover a wide range of topics; make sure a site caters to your target market. However, you should first determine if there is enough exposure within the niche you are looking for. If the number of active users or followers within a site's niche is particularly small, it may not warrant your time in marketing on that site.

SOCIAL NEWS: DO'S AND DONT'S

- The objective is to take advantage of social news sites without following any unfair practices. Some of these websites, like Digg, are controlled by algorithms. **DON'T** practice reciprocal 'digging' by joining Digg groups, known as crews, on a regular basis. Algorithms notice these patterns where people 'digg' each others stories and render them ineffective.

- People are always looking for unique content. **DO** ensure your story is newsworthy in order to attract readers' attention, gets votes and reaches the front page of the social news site.

- For a marketing campaign to succeed through social news sites, it is essential to build up a strong social network. **DO** interact with your network regularly so that you can create a personal rapport with users and build up a customer base.

- **DO** keep your finger on the pulse and remain aware of the changes in social media marketing.

- **DO** pay attention to feedback from customers and remain focused on your community.

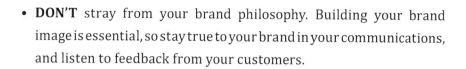

- **DON'T** stray from your brand philosophy. Building your brand image is essential, so stay true to your brand in your communications, and listen to feedback from your customers.

- **DO** become familiar with the culture of a particular community prior to signing up. Some communities may not like you mentioning other social news sites, so make sure you stay away from any controversies. For example, **DON'T** talk about Digg on the Reddit network. Both have different and distinct cultures and may politely ban you for any unfair practices.

- **DO** be patient as you become a part of a social news site—the right way. For example, voting for or Digging other peoples submissions is a part of building credibility and takes time. Social news sites are not for spamming, so **DO** select what you share and participate in carefully. Submitting stories or websites that nobody from social media visits or votes for will only help you to lose your credibility and trustworthiness.

- **DO** keep your marketing campaign subtle. Social news sites aren't meant for blatant marketing tactics. Going full steam with a promotional campaign on a website like Digg and Reddit will not work.

- Social news sites must be used to bring exposure to your organization's website. **DON'T** use these sites as a platform to slander your competition. That would only do your marketing campaign and reputation more harm than good.

- **DO** keep your social profile updated. Social news always needs fresh content as well as profiles that are relevant and active.

- Give social news sites time to work to your advantage. **DON'T** expect instant results. All good things are worth waiting for. What is most important at first is to update your content on a regular basis.

- **DO** understand the terms and rules of etiquette. Each site has its own set of etiquette that must be followed. Prior to submitting content on any social news community it is crucial to learn the culture and techniques in order to be accepted.

CULTUREQUOTE»

"FREQUENTLY CREATE USEFUL AND RELEVANT CONTENT"

SOCIAL NEWS: THE BENEFITS

An increasing number of organizations have found social news sites an effective way to promote their organizations.

Connecting with customers

Social news sites are ideal platforms organizations can use to build a personal rapport with their customers. This also helps organizations attract a bigger following, which leads to increased website traffic.

Listening to customer feedback

Customers that leave their feedback on these websites provide the perfect base for organizations to improve on their products or services and answer customer queries instantly.

Increasing web traffic

One of the main objectives of signing up on social news sites is to create links back your organization's website. Lead your target market directly where you want them and increase your reputation to search engines.

Building higher ranking in search engines

Since content on social news sites are based on user submission, search engines rank them higher in terms of quality and reputation. This gives organizations the opportunity to gain an edge in online visibility.

Build brand image

Social news sites give organizations the chance to build on their brand image and educate the public about their products or services. According to a recent study by Universal McCann, 45.8% of internet users have left

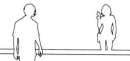

comments on social news sites. These websites have a large user-base that can provide massive exposure for an organization.

Creating informative content

This is what successful organizations do on social news sites. Creating informative and intriguing content that users find valuable increases a website's search visibility. Even users that only sign up and not necessarily convert to a sale are important, since it is the stepping stone to educating them on an organization's products or services.

Gaining additional publicity

Submissions that prove to be popular and receive a large number of votes lead to being featured on the social news site's homepage or featured as news items. Many organizations gain additional publicity by these methods.

Targeting specific audiences

Social news sites like Digg and Reddit give users the option of submitting stories in specific categories, even though they address a wide range of topics. Niche sites such as ShowHype and Sphinxx help target a specific audience.

Building authority and reputation

Social news sites related to an organization's particular niche allow for the implementation of highly targeted campaigns, which in turn helps the organization build a trusted and authoritative online presence.

Sharing thoughts and opinions

Social news sites offer a platform for communication and discussions.

Organizations that actively participate in these discussions add value to their brand as well as their website. For most organizations, a major chunk of monthly web traffic comes from these channels.

SOCIAL NEWS: SUCCESS STORIES

No organization can limit its online presence to banners and blogging. Social news sites provide powerful networking opportunities to reach out to potential customers. Reddit and Digg are among the top social news sites used by many organizations for their marketing campaigns.

Wired.com

In a recent experiment with Wired.com, Digg tracked changes on Wired's site to see what, if any, effect they would make. Originally the site had a 'share this' button but upon close inspection of traffic logs, it was discovered that the majority of traffic came from Digg, Yahoo! Buzz and StumbleUpon. So Wired.com pulled those buttons out of the 'share' widget and displayed them prominently. In doing this, they effectively told their audience "these are the sites we want you to focus on." The results were an increase from 500,000 clicks from Digg, to over a million.

Soapier.com

Founder Linda Nigro had grown the business from an internet wholesaler of soaps to a company with a full line of bath and spa products, a production facility and a retail store. She ran the business with the help of her daughter Erica Allen and son John, who's also a graphic artist.

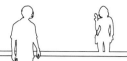

Tarpon Springs, Florida, is a tourist area and when the recession hit, the tourists disappeared, and so did much of Soapier's trade. Last December, Nigro told her daughter to find a job. Behind on her mortgage and other bills, Nigro decided to shut Soapier's production facility, close its retail store in Tarpon Springs and go back to producing only soap products in a home-based operation. At age 60, Nigro herself prepared to look for a part-time job, but that's when Nigro's son John posted a message on Reddit, a website that determines the popularity of members' postings using an upvote/downvote system. John's June 12 post explained the family's problems and offered Redditors a 25 percent off coupon. The Reddit community responded in unprecedented fashion. Within 24 hours the article received more than 700 upvotes, and Soapier received more than 200 orders from all over the world. In less than 48 hours, Soapier had received almost 400 orders, along with a slew of emails praising the look of the product, advice on the business and best wishes for the business. The tally has since topped 600 orders, and they're still coming in.

Burger King

Burger King is one of the major companies to excel at marketing through social media. One of the latest marketing strategies by the company is the use of Digg. The fast food chain attracts customers by placing ads promoting their $1 double cheeseburger for every search that yields no results on Digg. Included is an error message that says, "Looks like your search had a typo. Maybe you've got tiny hands? The beefy $1 Burger King Double Cheeseburger gives tiny hands some trouble, too." This type of marketing definitely creates new dimensions in web advertising and marketing.

"BE ACTIVE AND HELP OTHERS."

— JERRY ALLOCCA

SOCIAL NEWS: INTEGRATION WITH OTHER MEDIA

Social news sites are a great way to increase traffic to your website, with the ultimate goals of increasing branding, revenue and profits. Marketing directors who are new to social media must realize that there is no single social news or media platform, but a combination of platforms that lead to successful promotion of a brand. For the most part, social media changes the fundamental nature of customer relationships in relation to the brand.

Each component plays its part in any marketing initiatives that an organization undertakes. The key is to devise an appropriate strategy, review current marketing trends and then add an element of social media to the plan. Live events, webinars and virtual events can be shared on social news sites like Digg with messages sent through Twitter, drawing people's attention to the website. Considering today's trends, people love sharing information that they like on the web, which makes it essential for organizations to successfully integrate their social news with their website.

Social news sites like every other social media must be treated as an ingredient and not as a solitary tactic in the world of marketing. The bottom line is to lay out strategies first and then layout social programs in order to use it as an effective marketing tool.

SOCIAL NEWS: KEY TAKEAWAYS

- Determine your goals
- Research social news sites
- Determine users who influence others
- Set submission timelines and targets
- Interaction with other users
- Spread the word about social news sites
- Submitting stories
- Build a profile

SOCIAL NEWS: HOW DO I GET STARTED?

The following step-by-step guide will help you gain an understanding of the content that appeals to social communities and in turn, help determine your marketing strategy for social news.

Download a step-by-step workbook for developing your social news marketing plan.

Download the Connected Culture Social News Workbook FREE!

Visit: www.ConnectedCultureBook.com/freestuff
Enter in this code: news-workbook

WHAT IS SOCIAL BOOKMARKING?

Social bookmarking is an online service that helps internet users organize and manage their favorite bookmarks, which are direct links to online resources such as web pages, blog posts and videos. These bookmarks are stored in one place and can be shared with, and enjoyed by, other online users.

Descriptions may be added to these bookmarks in the form of metadata, so users can understand the content of the bookmarked resource without having to first open or download the link. Such descriptions may be in the form of comments, votes or keyword tags.

Some of the main benefits of using social bookmarking sites are that they are free to use and you can organize your bookmarks very efficiently. They can channel targeted traffic back to your site and allow you to build backlinks to your site. Building backlinks can help increase the page rank of your site, which results in higher rankings on search engine result pages.

The advantages

Not too long ago, saving links to websites was only possible in a web browser, by clicking the 'favorite' or 'bookmark' icon. However, these websites would only be bookmarked to your personal computer for you—and only you—to return to and view. Now, bookmarks can be saved on the web through social bookmarking websites, which makes them easy to share. This gives like-minded individuals the opportunity to join and create new communities that influence the way people search.

Social bookmarking allows users to target what they want to see. These sites recently added lists and popular links which ensure that the information available is updated. Users no longer need to go through numerous pages on search engines in order to find something specific which may be available on social bookmarking sites. All that users need to do is choose a tag or category within a social bookmarking site that matches their interest and find the most popular websites relevant to their search.

The most important aspect of social bookmarking? Building backlinks to your web pages and increasing the reputation of those pages in search engines.

"BUILDING BACKLINKS TO YOUR WEBSITE DRIVES TRAFFIC AND HELPS SEO."

— JERRY ALLOCCA

SOCIAL BOOKMARKING: TOP CHOICES

Explore the most popular social bookmarking sites and see which platforms offer your organization the best fit. As with other social media sites, there are some sites specific to social bookmarking and others that serve a dual purpose. For example, Twitter is a popular social microblogging site but can also be used as a social bookmarking site.

Delicious (formerly known as del.icio.us)

Delicious is a free social bookmarking site that allows users to bookmark their favorite content on the web. In this way, users can determine the popularity of the content they search for and go directly to those resources. The site acts as a huge database with plenty of web links. Users can be certain of finding the latest and most trendy content. Delicious has an easy-to-use interface and allows users to promote links to their own blogs and websites.

StumbleUpon

StumbleUpon is a popular social bookmarking site which marketers tend to choose because of its viral nature. When searching, all you need to do is put in the keyword and click the 'stumble' icon. The website fetches relevant results much like search engines do, in a refined manner. StumbleUpon allows users to rate web pages, videos and photos. The site also features a toolbar that can be added to your own browser. This enables you to automatically link to content that interests you and that you can vote on or rate.

Tweetmeme

Tweetmeme, among the top social bookmarking sites, evaluates links on Twitter to determine the most popular. These links are categorized, making it easier for users to search for specific websites of interest. The site has a Tweetmeme icon to tweet about new content, which is posted on Twitter. The stories with the most tweets make it to the front page of the website.

Yahoo! Buzz

Yahoo! Buzz combines social networking and bookmarking, similar to social news sites like Digg. The site allows Yahoo users to post links to their own content as well as vote for stories. Those stories that manage a high rating are featured on Yahoo's home page, which results in a significant amount of exposure (and more traffic) for the website publishing the story. One of the major differences between Buzz and other sites is that, on Buzz, stories can only be published with approval from Yahoo. Users cannot submit their own stories directly but can only vote on stories provided by Yahoo! Buzz.

Mixx

Mixx is a popular social media site that combines bookmarking, news and networking. The site allows users to submit and find content based on interest and location. Mixx users can interact with each other and share their common interests. Content that is featured on Mixx comes from various sources such as news services and includes videos, images and other forms of content. Users are allowed to submit items from their own website, as well.

OK, SO WHICH ONE DO I CHOOSE?

Social bookmarking sites are a good way to increase you organization's online exposure by driving traffic to your website. Choosing the right social bookmarking site may take some research, especially when it comes to marketing your organization's products or services. Many of the sites are similar, but each one has its own unique features. Among the factors to consider are the type of audience the site attracts and the relevance of the subject matter. In addition, consider whether the site features a "dofollow" link so that users are allowed to follow you. It is essential to add bookmarking widgets to your blog so that others can recommend and share it.

Check out a few social bookmarking sites and see what you think of them. You may need to consider becoming a member on a couple of sites. Some sites allow you to submit stories and search without having to sign up. These sites may be ideal to start with until you can determine what works best for your type of marketing strategy.

One of the most important things on social bookmarking sites is to gather votes. These votes increase the chances of driving traffic to your website. It is important to choose a site that allows backlinks to your blogs, articles, websites and videos. Some sites give a 'no-follow' link to your blogs or websites, which will not help increase your exposure in search engines. Sites like Delicious have a 'dofollow' link which is good if you want to optimize your website for search engines.

With technology constantly evolving and markets changing, it is necessary to keep a close watch on the leading social bookmarking sites and monitor your progress. This makes it easy to finally focus on one or two that work best for your marketing campaign.

SOCIAL BOOKMARKING: DO'S AND DON'TS

- Social bookmarking is a form of interaction and what you say and do reflects on your organization's profile. **DO** maintain etiquette in order to be accepted by online communities and build your brand image.

- It is important to create and maintain interest so that users are attracted to your website. **DO** target the right demographic and generate a profile that includes information that appeals to them.

- Linking is an important aspect of bookmarking. **DO** add links to and from popular bookmarking sites with the help of bookmarking tools in order to increase online traffic.

- When posting content and adding bookmarks that are informative and interesting, they need to be placed in the right category. **DO** make sure you join the right category, or your marketing efforts may be in vain. **DO** join sites that have unique categories so you can find the right fit.

- To use social bookmarking sites to your advantage you need to remain active and add to the conversation. **DO** make it a point to respond to comments and exchange ideas with other users. A personal approach to business always works and will significantly increase your traffic and conversion rate. Establishing contacts will help you win votes and bring visitors to your website.

- **DO** arouse interest in users by using catchy titles, and **DO** add interesting facts in your first paragraph. This is a great way to get users to bookmark your page.

- **DO** add bookmarks throughout the week at fixed intervals rather than all in one day.

- **DO** use social bookmarking sites that are able to direct traffic to your site.

- **DON'T** make the mistake of using automated software, which is the quickest way to drive people away. Many automated software programs contain malware, which is malicious software designed to secretly access a computer system without the owner's informed consent and can ruin your online reputation in an instant. Most sites do not allow automated entries with programs and scripting techniques like captchas, ensuring that users post only quality submissions.

- **DO** send relevant content that is specific to the group you're communicating with. Sending the same content to all the groups you join will result in your organization being banned.

- **DO** keep reading the front page of social bookmarking sites to determine what active users want to read about and what they share.

SOCIAL BOOKMARKING: THE BENEFITS

When combined with other marketing strategies, organizations have found social bookmarking sites to be an effective way of marketing their products and services by increasing traffic and growing brand recognition.

Generating traffic

Social bookmarking sites are good vehicles for gaining online exposure. When useful content is submitted to these sites they are guaranteed to send targeted traffic to your organization's website.

Personal branding

Websites like StumbleUpon and Delicious give your organization the opportunity to develop its own page on their site. This is a great way to develop a profile that can be used to post links to your organization's website and publish content in any niche.

Getting noticed by search engines

Search engines easily index pages that are submitted to popular sites like StumbleUpon, Delicious and others. This not only helps increase online exposure but also is an ideal way to build your organization's brand image.

Targeted traffic

Social bookmarking sites allow users to build on a personal page. In addition, they allow links to websites, which is a cost effective way of gaining higher ranks on search engines. Social bookmarking sites offer quality traffic rather than just quantity. Information stored on these sites is well organized, which makes them search engine friendly. Therefore, whenever users search for specific information, search engines return a significant amount of results from social bookmarking sites.

Access to new business resources

Social bookmarking sites allow organizations to gain access to new business resources. The information can be used to stay on top of your industry and alter marketing strategies accordingly.

Listening to customer feedback

Customers are able to leave comments and vote on posts, presenting the ideal opportunity for organizations to gather information on what is being said about their products or services.

Strengthening business relationships

By interacting on social bookmarking sites, organizations have the chance to build up better business contacts through sharing of information, voting and adding comments. It is easy to collaborate with partners to spread the word about your organization's products or services through social bookmarking sites.

Creating libraries of information

Social bookmarking sites help users to create libraries of information that can be sorted and shared with others. This is useful when it comes to dealing with a variety of content on a daily basis.

Website branding

Branding your website is an important part of building a brand image. Social bookmarking sites help to brand your organization's website as long as they choose the right niche and build appropriate tags and keywords. Submitting quality content to social bookmarking sites attracts the attention of other members and makes them relate to your organization's website.

SOCIAL BOOKMARKING: SUCCESS STORIES

Chevrolet

One of the top companies to make use of social bookmarking sites like Delicious and Twitter is Chevrolet. Adam Denison is the company's PR person for models including Corvette, Camaro, Impala and HHR. Apart from managing queries from the media, Denison tweets about them and provides regular updates with interesting news and photos for automobile enthusiasts. Denison continues to gather a large following for the company on Twitter, who are all talking about Chevrolet's cars.

Kodak

Kodak has a major presence on most popular social media sites including Delicious and Twitter. The company's chief blogger handles corporate blogs, microblogs and bookmarking sites. Their Twitter and Delicious accounts are used to respond to customer queries, gain valuable feedback, drive more traffic to their site and monitor conversations about what is happening in the industry. The company's chief blogger shares tips and news about photography and printing with other users. The main objective of using these platforms is to increase awareness of Kodak products and keep people informed of the latest from the company. Any special deals are also passed on through regular tweets.

Isaac Marion

Isaac Marion was a Seattle-based blogger and writer who was unknown in 2008, until his short story "I Am a Zombie Filled with Love" was distributed on his website and purchased by about 100 readers. The story was also reviewed by a lot of users on the StumbleUpon network, and it was so highly rated that Cori Stern, a Hollywood screenwriter and producer, literally "stumbled upon" the story and instantly thought it would make a great movie.

From there Stern introduced Marion's work to her colleagues and the story was so good that it turned into a movie deal. Had Stern not stumbled upon the story, none of this would have been possible. The story speaks to how powerful social bookmarking and crowd-sourcing sites can be.

SOCIAL BOOKMARKING: INTEGRATION WITH OTHER MEDIA

One of the main advantages of social bookmarking sites is that they also allow organizations to integrate their websites with other social media sites. Everyone finds the need to categorize and organize content, and these sites provide the necessary tools to do so. Several tools are available to allow posts to be integrated using one platform. Since link building is an essential part of any online marketing campaign, it is essential to integrate as many social networks as possible on your web page or blog.

Social media marketing involves a combination of various platforms, which is why you need to understand each component prior to using it in your marketing initiatives. To begin with, you need to determine what search terms your organization needs to utilize and integrate them into the profiles on social bookmarking sites. Images can also be uploaded and shared while links to social profiles in display ads must be included.

Earlier, many organizations shied away from social media marketing due to the fear of losing control over their message and brand image.

However, integrating traditional marketing strategies with social media can help marketers guide the message instead of control it. This is due to the influence and reach of social media and bookmarking sites in particular. Eventually, it is up to customers to decide what image an organization's brand is defined as.

SOCIAL BOOKMARKING: KEY TAKEAWAYS

- Create accounts
- Download tools and buttons
- Join relevant communities
- Create categories
- Submit links
- Keep networking

SOCIAL BOOKMARKING: HOW DO I GET STARTED?

Using social bookmarking sites for marketing is a simple task once you determine sites that suit your organization's marketing requirements. For those just starting out in the world of social bookmarking, the following workbook can lead you to success.

Download a step-by-step workbook for developing your social bookmarking marketing plan.

Download the Connected Culture Social Bookmarking Workbook FREE!

Visit: www.ConnectedCultureBook.com/freestuff
Enter in this code: bookmarking-workbook

SECTION FOUR:
STAYING CONNECTED

What does it mean to stay connected?

It doesn't matter whether you are a business professional, small business owner, or the marketing director of a large organization, you still need to network and stay connected with colleagues, customers and associates. Thanks to the internet and various forms of social media, staying connected is easy today. You can be in your car, sitting in your office, or enjoying a pleasure trip at the seaside and still be in constant touch with associates and colleagues across the world. All this is possible through mobile communication, instant messaging, email, social networking sites like Facebook, LinkedIn and Twitter, chats, video conferencing, photo sharing, wall-to-wall posts and much more. Social networking especially has had a significant impact on the mobile market.

Cell phones have become an extension of online networking. Cellular social networking has spread rapidly in areas with a lower number of internet users and a higher number of cell phone users. The internet-integrated smart phone helps us to reach out to others anywhere, even when there's no personal computer in sight. Most smart phones are installed with business applications that allow users to work even while commuting. Managing bank accounts, transferring funds, getting in touch with employees to make final changes for your corporate presentation, or fine tuning a marketing strategy is all possible while on the move. Smart phones have greater built-in functionality to help users remain organized. These handsets function as personal organizers with automatic reminders and contact lists. Smart phones enable users to take notes, edit, and review contacts and documents while away from the office. Most importantly, these phones allow you to have information at your fingertips with easy access to maps and directions, news coverage, alerts and traffic information to keep you one step ahead. Better functionality, information sharing and faster communication are the distinct characteristics of smart phone devices that help users stay connected.

Organizations have to give thanks to technology for the ability to stay connected with customers 24/7. Social media sites help organizations build up a brand image and implement marketing strategies without having to spend colossal amounts on advertising and marketing campaigns. Plus, almost every employee can be trained to utilize social media and further their organization's presence online. Social media sites enable you to stay connected with customers, gather and share knowledge, collect data on customer trends, respond to comments, revise marketing strategies and business plans and much more. This knowledge can be transmitted from one person to another in a matter of minutes whether a person is online or not.

STAYING CONNECTED: THE DEVICES

Smart Phones

Smart phones are mobile devices that include more applications and online functions than traditional cell phones. Smart phones function similar to a mini computer or any other portable digital device that you can carry any place you go. Besides regular text messaging, these phones allow users to send emails, manage documents, visit websites, browse for information, take photos and video, record audio, take dictation, play games and much more. The applications are only limited by your imagination. Smart phones can be attached to PCs and laptops in order to share documents and applications. Undoubtedly, these devices make life easier, which is why these tiny gadgets demand a price. Smart phones include an operating system, software and other applications, email messaging, internet access, PC sharing abilities and in some cases, a touch screen and voice command. Some of the more popular smart phones are iPhones from Apple, Research in Motion RIM Blackberry, Motorola Droid, Palm's Treo and Nokia E63, to name a few.

iPhone from Apple

One of the leaders in smart phone technology is the iPhone from Apple. These phones are designed to run on the iPhone operating system. Users can make a call by voice command or by simply pointing at a name in the address book, select and listen to voicemail messages, and sync contacts from a PC, Mac or hosted web service like Exchange from Microsoft and MobileMe from Apple. Apart from its sleek, attractive looks, the iPhone is a personal computer, digital and video camera, music (iPod) player and much more. As long as your mobile service provider gives you high quality internet access, this device is among the most powerful communications tools. Among the latest iPhones to hit the market is the iPhone 4, which includes a higher-resolution screen for crisper and brighter images and videos, a faster processor, and front-facing camera for video calls that can be made to other iPhone users over Wi-Fi. When you need to type something, a virtual keyboard appears and allows you to input data.

You can synchronize your iPhone wirelessly using services like Exchange or MobileMe, or by physically connecting it to your PC or Mac. This enables you to seamlessly integrate important contacts, calendar and all necessary information, so you can access what you need, when you need it, wherever you are.

iPhone applications (Apps)

Many professionals, including organizations, have turned to iPhones due to the number of easy-to-use business applications, or "apps," these smart phones have to offer. It is easy to monitor income and expenses, organize schedules, tasks and contacts, and convert currency, with the help of these apps.

There are thousands of iPhone apps available. Among them are Facetime, a built-in application that allows users to make a video phone call (to other iPhone 4 users), so you can talk to other people and see them as well thanks to its dual camera, one on each side. Facetime or video calls bring about a whole new way of communicating and connecting with someone. Most of us are not used to being able to see the person you are talking to on the phone, but as I said in the beginning of this book, the world has changed in a big way.

Task2Gather is another application that maintains business, personal and family tasks. You can organize tasks, and share them with iPhone and other users, as well. Each task can be divided into subtasks and delegated accordingly. Another application ideal for contact management is LinkedIn for iPhone. This application enables you to manage your contacts on social networks so the contacts themselves keep their information current and you automatically get their latest information. You can add people and communicate with your connections, as well.

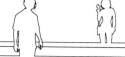

BlackBerry RIM

BlackBerry has been one of the most successful smart phones for a long time. Many professionals, including organizations large and small, have turned to BlackBerry to stay connected because of its functionality. The integrated software enables you to access a variety of communication services. You can use the BlackBerry for emails, internet access, phone capabilities, loading and reading maps, running numerous applications, playing games and much more. Included are a media player and camera, which makes the BlackBerry much more than just a powerful communication tool.

The BlackBerry can use GPS (Global Positioning System), a technology based on satellite communication, to track locations easily. Instant messaging services, and email help you keep in touch while you are on the move. BlackBerry has social networking capabilities, which is a major attraction for those who need to stay connected at all times. These smart phones are designed with the QWERTY style keyboard or SureType® keyboard technology, making it easy to type. Some models include a trackball for easy navigation.

BlackBerry applications

There are several applications available for BlackBerry including social networking applications for Facebook, Twitter, Flickr, MySpace and more. Instant messaging applications include BlackBerry Messenger with a chat style layout. The application allows chat anywhere, anytime, and includes the ability to send and receive messages. The application allows you to share photos and videos with multiple contacts. TwitterBerry is an application that enables BlackBerry users to send out Twitter updates quickly, and view and respond to messages. Most applications require an unlimited data plan from the provider.

Google phone products

Internet search engine giant Google has a number of products for phones. All these products can be accessed through the mobile device's browser. Blogger Mobile is an application that allows you to update blogs on Blogger from your mobile device. Users can add events to a personal calendar on a mobile device and display a list of events through Google Calendar. To view and share photo albums stored online on Picasa, Google has an application called Picasa Web Albums. Google also provides a mobile application to access and download Gmail messages. The application allows you to access your Gmail account from a mobile device by using a mobile web browser. Google Mobile Search is another application that allows you to search web pages including local listings, images and more.

Tablet PCs

As technology-related products continue to evolve, Tablet PCs with touch-screen technology continue to enter the market at a steady pace.

iPad

Among the latest tablet computers designed by Apple is the iPad. This touch-screen device is an ideal platform for audio and visual presentations including books, movies, games, music, PowerPoint presentations (or Keynote) and any web content (unless it contains Flash technology). The iPad uses the same operating system as the iPhone. It features a multi-touch display and uses a Wi-Fi or 3G connection for internet access.

iPod Touch

The iPod Touch is similar to an iPhone without the capabilities of a phone. The device is among the best music and video players and is a great gaming device as well. Apart from two cameras, the iPod Touch also includes a GameCenter that allows users to play games socially with other users and friends. In terms of software and applications, the iPod Touch includes a social networking feature for iTunes 10.

STAYING CONNECTED: THE PLATFORMS

Social networking – Facebook

Facebook, the top social networking platform, includes a popular mobile application. Rather than post URLs on TV commercials to encourage people to visit a website, it is easier to ask them to follow your organization on Facebook. The social networking site has great potential for organizations to expand their customer base and build their brand image. Announcing special deals, responding to customer queries, and staying connected are just a few things that organizations can accomplish through this platform. The website features Facebook Marketing Solutions, a page run by employees of Facebook to help marketers share with users and create movements in the community.

Social blogging – WordPress

WordPress is an easy-to-use social blogging platform that can be used on a mobile device. The website has an active community that makes it one of the best marketing tools for organizations. Setting up blogs through WordPress is a great way to drive traffic to a website. Organizations have the option of adding a simple page on WordPress where prospective clients can enter their contact details, which makes it a great way to build up a prospective client database. Organizations can blog about their products, services and news relevant to their industry by setting up WordPress pages. This, in return, increases their online exposure by driving traffic to their website.

Social microblogging – Twitter

Twitter is the leading microblogging platform, and has plenty of great features that organizations can utilize on the go. One of the biggest advantages is that it connects people in real time. Even though messages can only be up to 140 characters long, they have a far reaching effect since messages can be sent via computers or cellular phones. Marketing directors find this a convenient tool to keep customers informed about their products, keep them engaged in conversations and build up new relationships. Twitter is definitely one of the most cost effective and efficient ways to implement a marketing strategy.

Social videos - YouTube

Visual media is one of the most effective ways to launch an advertising or marketing campaign. Social video sharing sites like YouTube allow users to upload videos and share it with the world. The video sharing site is visited by thousands every day, making it easy for organizations to promote their products or services by uploading videos to the site from their mobile device. In this way, marketers are able to increase traffic to their website. Any video that goes viral can result in a significant amount of traffic to an organization's website. In addition, organizations create groups in order to increase their chances of potential clients visiting their websites.

Social photos - Flickr

The advancements in mobile technology have made it possible to take photos and share them instantly. Social photo sharing sites like Flickr hosts over 5 billion images, which makes it an ideal platform for organizations to upload images related to their products or services and share them with a large audience. Along with digital images, links to blogs can be embedded, which ultimately leads to visitors to an organization's website.

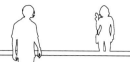

Social news – Digg

Social news sites are also powerful marketing tools for organizations to take advantage of viral marketing. Platforms like Digg help to attract the attention of customers by hosting news on the website, which in turn results in greater web exposure for the sites that generate the news stories. Organizations can share content relevant to their industry. Users are allowed to vote on newsworthy stories, and stories that gather the highest votes make it to the front page of Digg. Appearing on Digg's front page will drive more traffic to your site.

Social bookmarking – Delicious

Social bookmarking is also an integral part of social networking with websites like Delicious (formerly known as del.icio.us) helping marketers increase their chances of reaching out to a larger audience. Delicious allows users to bookmark content that appeals to them on the web. In addition, the website allows users to share links to their own blogs and websites, which is ideal for marketers to implement as part of their organization's search engine optimization strategies. Users are allowed to vote, which is what organizations take advantage of in a bid to build up their online presence.

Text messaging

A growing number of organizations have been using text messaging in order to engage in a dialogue with their customers. It is an easy way for customers to learn more about a product by simply sending a short message to which the organization sends an instant reply. For example, a company that sells smart phones can ask users to send a short message such as "Review iPhone," in order to receive details about the iPhone. Through text messaging, organizations are able to let customers place orders and review their order status. In addition, it is also used to help keep customers informed about the availability of a product or service. One of the most important aspects of text messaging is that organizations are in a position to answer customer queries regarding location of their stores and other relevant information. Similar to messages that are relayed on Twitter, text messaging is used to inform customers about special deals and discounts that are periodically available.

Email

Email marketing is an effective way for organizations to remain connected with customers. For an organization, it is an easy way to launch a promotional campaign to convince existing customers to make another purchase, as well as acquire new customers from referrals and sharing. Among the main objectives of email marketing is to enhance customer relationships and encourage customer loyalty. This type of marketing is popular because it is cheaper than most other forms of communication. Email messages are delivered directly to people, unlike websites where people need to visit it in order to read a message.

Search engines

Search engine marketing, or SEM, is an essential element of website promotion. This helps organizations get found when people search for them by increasing their visibility in search engine result pages (SERPs). An organization's website needs to be fully optimized in order to become search engine friendly and referable. This includes the use of keywords and key phrases that people use when they are looking for information through search engines such as Google, Yahoo and Bing. As of February, 2010, over 100 billion people every month use search engines to find products, which is one of the main reasons that search engine marketing is important.

SEM is one of the most cost effective marketing tools available considering there are 34,000 searches per second on Google alone. That's 3 billion searches per day, or 88 billion per month (figures rounded; figures complied by searchengineland.com are accurate as of February 2010.) When combining only the 3 major search engines—Google, Yahoo and Bing—there are over 100 billion searches per month...and it's not slowing down anytime soon, especially with mobile search on the rise. SEM enables organizations to gather statistics from analytical software in order to determine the effectiveness of an ad campaign. In addition, it is the best way to attract customers that are looking for specific products on a search engine.

STAYING CONNECTED: WHAT YOU SHOULD KNOW

It is essential for any organization to remain in constant touch with existing customers, as well as utilize existing technologies such as communications and networking, to implement their marketing strategies effectively. That's why it's important to make use of social media platforms, such as the ones I mentioned in the section above. These platforms enhance brand images and increase web presence, as well.

Networking, blogging, microblogging, video sharing, photo sharing, news sharing and social bookmarking, as well as email and SEM, are all essential elements that play an important role in any online marketing strategy. Organizations have a number of devices at their disposal, like the iPhone and BlackBerry smart phones, to help them stay connected with customers and attract new ones. Both of these mobile devices are valuable marketing tools since they are portable and include many social networking features. It is easy to send text messages, emails, manage documents, and much more through smart phones, making them effective tools to stay connected.

The convenience that wireless networks bring to organizations cannot be ignored. Staying connected leads to an increase in productivity and is one of the best ways to boost customer relationships by providing better customer service. However, it is important for a marketing director to choose a platform that suits their marketing strategy best. Moreover, social media platforms and smart phone devices must be treated as a part of any marketing strategy and cannot be used individually in order to be effective. It is advisable to assess your organization's marketing needs and goals and then move on to understanding various technologies and their capabilities before implementing a marketing plan. In the effort to stay connected, it is also important to take care of security issues in order to ensure the safety of your customers as well as your organization's sensitive data.

SECTION FIVE:
DIS-CONNECTING

Social media is all about friendships and relationships. And just like any other relationship, online friendships require effort and cultivation on both sides. If you start to fall behind on your friendships and stop putting forth an effort, then you start to dis-connect.

HERE ARE SOME SITUATIONS THAT MAY INDICATE YOU ARE BEGINNING TO DIS-CONNECT:

Situation: You are not maintaining the relationship

Any good relationship requires active participation on both sides. If you neglect to respond to your customers' inquiries or comments, or fail to reciprocate, you are not playing an active role in that relationship. You may be dis-connecting. Devoting some time to the relationship to keep the lines of communication open will prevent you from losing your connection with your associates and customers.

Situation: You put a connection on probation

You may consider dis-connecting if you feel that you need to put one of your connections on probation. You may have adjusted your feed settings to avoid seeing certain connections' feeds. You could be tired of seeing their daily activities broadcasted moment by moment, but still like to talk to them from time to time. Or maybe they are being salesy, trying to advertise in comments or steer attention away from your group. Whatever your reason may be, if you filter out their feeds, then you may be on the road to dis-connecting. Before you cut that person out of your network, take a moment to think about whether dis-connecting with that person will have a negative impact on your relationship, or if you would both be better off moving on. If there's something worth working out, then give it a try.

Situation: You choose to ignore incoming messages, or someone ignores yours

If you are not interacting with a connection through messages, comments or through their status updates, you need to consider if dis-connecting will be beneficial for both of you. Conversely, think about others who have not interacted with you. Is there anyone that ignores your messages? Is there anyone who does not interact online with you in the way you would hope? You may need to evaluate the relationship and decide if this person is worth having in your network and if you want to continue to pursue or maintain the relationship.

Situation: You feel like it is time to move on

Have you ever thought about completely cutting someone out of your network? Sometimes adjusting a feed setting just isn't enough and dis-connecting seems like the better option. You could remove that person from your friend list and not tell them. Or you could send them a message to explain why you have deleted that person from your network.

Situation: You don't accept someone's friend request

You may have an invitation to connect in your inbox, and you may want to further qualify that invitation. Perhaps it's a competitor, or an ex-employee you're not sure you can trust. You could either choose to ignore that request, or to reach out and establish a line of communication. Send an email or message. Offer to chat over the phone.

Situation: You decide to totally leave a social network

There is nothing forcing you to continue to participate in a social network. You can leave at any time. The average social networker has approximately 100 people on their connection list. Leaving that network and deleting your account wipes out all of the connections that you have created and cultivated on that site, and at that point you have dis-connected with those people all at once. Rather than totally leaving the network, you may want to consider dis-connecting with certain people while devoting more time to the people with whom you have valuable interactions. Another option is to make one final post informing people that you will no longer be actively maintaining this social profile, and direct them to another site where you want them to follow you.

What is the right choice?

Dis-connecting online only takes a few clicks of a mouse button. Depending on your relationship with the other person who is currently in your online network, dis-connecting could have varying results. Think about the implications before you make the choice.

- Is your organization better off without the relationship?
- Will there be feelings of rejection?
- Will it have a positive or negative impact on your organization's brand image?
- Will it affect your personal life?

Think before you click the "hide", "ignore" or "delete" button. Decide carefully whether or not it benefits both of you to keep the connection or if you should be dis-connected.

SECTION SIX:
APPLYING IT ALL

Knowledge is essential, but the only way you will really learn anything and see any measurable results is practical application of knowledge. So go out and apply the principles in this book that make the most sense for your organization and its goals. Download the workbooks and create your own step-by-step plans. And most importantly, have fun doing it. I wish you all the best on your journey, and if you ever need help along your path feel free to drop me a line at **Jerry@CORE.bz.**

- JERRY ALLOCCA

ABOUT THE AUTHOR

Jerry Allocca is the founder of CORE Interactive, and creator of the Connected Culture Series of Training and Accountability Programs. He leads an award-winning team of Internet specialists and over the years has come to be recognized as an internet and marketing guru. Jerry's passion is to help people connect online.

Jerry is a frequent industry speaker on such topics as websites, interactive marketing and social media. He has taken his many years of internet marketing experience and has used that knowledge to write *Connected Culture.* It is the first book to comprehensively bridge the marketing gap between your organization and today's digital generation.

For more information visit
www.JerryAllocca.com
or google **"Jerry Allocca".**

FREE STUFF

Here's a list of all the free stuff offered in this book, consolidated into one place for your convenience.

Visit www.ConnectedCultureBook.com/freestuff

Enter the following codes to download the step-by-step workbooks to help you get started in the world of digital media:

> **website-workbook**
>
> **email-workbook**
>
> **txt-workbook**
>
> **sem-workbook**
>
> **blogging-workbook**
>
> **microblogging-workbook**
>
> **networking-workbook**
>
> **videos-workbook**
>
> **photos-workbook**
>
> **news-workbook**
>
> **bookmarking-workbook**

CONNECTED CULTURE: TRAINING AND ACCOUNTABILITY PROGRAMS

Connected Culture Training and Accountability Programs are available as an integrated and interactive learning solution that can take place in or out of your office.

Programs include:

- Participant workbooks
- Computer lab training
- Web meeting training
- e-learning reinforcement
- Help and support

Call 516.719.6235 or
visit www.connectedculturebook.com
for more information.

NOTES:

Made in the USA
Charleston, SC
01 April 2011